"Porn addicts are, unfort
days. And in the Christiai
is no lack of would-be the
Gardner stands heads-and shoulders above the rest in
this grassroots movement. His ruthless desire to be, first
of all, faithful to the revealed truth of the Bible, and second, practically helpful to men entrenched in lust is what
enables him to so easily marry doctrine with down-to-earth counsel. Brian has spent years helping the men in
his church pursue real sexual integrity, and that wisdom
comes out in this well-researched book. More than this,
Brian is a real trophy of God's costly grace. He unabashedly shares with his readers about the squalor of the far
country from where the Father called him, and the joy of
freedom he enjoys as a child of the living God. I heartily
recommend this book."

Luke Gilkerson, Internet Community Manager,
Covenant Eyes

"With pornography swamping the church today like a
tidal wave, the need for strong, pointed instruction is
intense. Brian Gardner has mined his extensive experience and study in this field to bring us a highly useful
book for men and women suffering defeat in their lives
because of pornography. Get this book to the people in
your church who need it. Even consider group study
using the helpful group discussion questions provided."

Dennis McCallum, Lead Pastor, Xenos Christian
Fellowship and author, *Organic Discipleship*, *Satan
and His Kingdom*, and *Members of One Another*.

"I highly recommend Brian Gardner's *Porn Free* as a book that is authentic, biblical, and gospel-centered. Gardner's honesty and practicality make the book a must read for anyone wanting to know more about the struggle with pornography and how to experience hope and healing through a relationship with Jesus Christ."

Joe Bucha, speaker and licensed professional counselor

"It was a joy to review Brian Gardner's much-needed book, *Porn Free: Finding Renewal through Truth and Community*. The foundation on God's Grace sets the hopeful tone that will help men persevere with this most challenging arena. He has done a marvelous job of combining a strong scriptural foundation with personal disclosure, well-chosen outside sources, and provocative discussion questions. What a gift for groups of men who embrace their need for sexual integrity! For men who are committed to "walk the walk" in becoming more Christ-like in all areas of their lives, here is a great resource to help them appropriate God's Grace in the sexual arena. Brian has created a work that should prove to be a blessing to the men who accept the challenge of working through it and to the women and families God has (or will) bless them with."

Ronald J. Olah, PhD, Psychologist

PORN FREE

FINDING RENEWAL
THROUGH TRUTH AND COMMUNITY

Brian W. Gardner

Porn Free:
Finding Renewal through Truth and Community

Copyright © 2011 Brian W. Gardner

Published by Costly Grace Media, Worthington, Ohio
www.costlygracemedia.com

Italics in biblical quotes indicate emphasis added.

Book Design: Brian Gardner
Cover Design: Dave Schulz and Brian Gardner

ISBN: 978-0-9840335-0-8

Table of Contents

Introduction   vii

1   The Problem with Porn   17

2   My Problem with Porn   37

3   The False Solution   59

4   Costly Grace   75

5   All of Life is Repentance   95

6   A Mind Renewed   113

7   Living in the Light of Community   131

8   The Battle   149

9   Temptation and Failure   167

10   Real Men, Real Relationships   187

11   The Practice of Delight   203

12   Our Future Hope   219

Bibliography   235

Introduction

Porn Free: Finding Renewal through Truth and Community is for people who are seeking freedom from sexual sin. The main emphasis of this book is on gaining freedom from the trap of pornography. The essential content of this book can also be applied to other areas of sexual sin, such as masturbation and fantasy, cybersex in chat rooms, serial sexual relationships, fetishes, same-sex desires, and so forth.

For the purposes of this book, it's not the particular expression of sexual brokenness that is the issue. The reality is that most of us are sexually broken in one way or another. For some of us, this has led to addiction, shame, and defeat. If any of those words describe you, or someone you are trying to help, then this book is for you. This book is written from a biblical Christian perspective. While it is possible to stop using pornography without knowing God, "there is salvation in no one else, for there is no other name under heaven given among men by which we must be saved." (Acts 4:12) Only by the power of Christ working in our lives can we have real and lasting victory over sin.

My Story

I saw my first pornography when I was 9 or 10 years old. Even before that I always had a fascination with sex. The pages of *National Geographic* were engrossing reading;

a crude drawing in a medical dictionary revealed mysteries to me. Growing up in the 60's didn't afford many opportunities for access to explicit material; those were still well hidden behind counters or locked up in the seamiest of adult bookstores. However, I never missed an opportunity to expand my education, and by the time I was in Jr. High school I was buying and selling naked pictures of housewives from black and white "sun lovers" magazines and single frames from an 8mm video that could only be discerned under a microscope.

I kept a discreet relationship with *Playboy* in high school and *Penthouse* in college. After I became a Christian in 1974 I stopped looking at porn, but continued with fantasy and masturbation. When I got married I assumed that I would give it all up for good. It was only a couple of months into my marriage before I went to the local convenience store to get a pornographic magazine for the first time. At the time I didn't think much of it, even though the withering look from the elderly sales lady made me feel ashamed. I kept that magazine hidden in the bottom of the closet, and soon others joined it. When I was alone in our apartment, I would take them out and use them. Still, it wasn't until many years later that what was a passing fancy became an obsession. The agent of my demise was the Internet.

As a software developer I was an early adopter of the Internet, getting involved long before the World Wide Web became synonymous with it. Though I had other interests, getting access to pictures of naked women was at the heart of my fixation. By the early 90's I was collecting and consuming porn at an alarming rate. I was still married, had two children, a good job, and was teaching the Bible as well as leading home groups. I was living a double life. I was addicted.

I tried to stop, but the power to do so seemed out of reach. When I tried to approach God about my problem I felt guilt and shame. I would promise to do better and fail within days, or hours, or even minutes. I didn't want to share my problem because I knew that it could cost me my ministry and my place in the church. I was respected, so that would be lost too. My wife would be hurt and angry. I decided I could stop on my own, without telling anyone. I would stop – tomorrow. One more look wouldn't hurt.

I thought that God couldn't help me with my porn problem, but as I look back on it now I realize that I really didn't want him to. I wanted to keep God compartmentalized. I wanted God to help me serve and teach and share with others, but I didn't want him involved with all of my life. All the while I was slipping away from him, he was patiently waiting for me to acknowledge him as my Lord, to be won over by his love. He waited for years. Finally, the pressure of conviction overwhelmed me. I acknowledged my sin, received his forgiveness, and came clean to my wife and friends that I had betrayed with my deceit. I began to try to find out what it meant to live in the light, and began the hard road of recovery.

There is much more to my story, and the pages of this book tell some of the rest of it. What I want to say at this point is that I have talked to hundreds of men who have had a very similar experience. Are you one of them? There is hope for you. My God loves you, and he is greater than your sin and failure, and he has a way for you to find renewal.

Thesis

Freedom from the power of sexual sin can be yours. No matter what you've done, or how long you've been doing it, you can experience real transformation and true freedom. How can this be? It's what God wants for you. Many approaches to this problem focus on controlling yourself and working to stop sinful behavior. Most Christian books on this topic take that approach. Stop looking at porn, stop having serial sexual affairs, stop going to strip clubs, massage parlors and prostitutes, stop flirting, lusting, and masturbating! Much of my own journey was like this, trying to stop. I joined 12-step groups, I used behavioral modification techniques such as wearing a very thick rubber band around my wrist and snapping it hard when I would have a lustful thought. I focused almost entirely on how to "just stop it".

Even though these approaches can be helpful, they do not bring freedom. As I struggled to control my sexual desires, a verse in Paul's letter to the Galatians kept sticking in my mind: "live by the Spirit, and you will not gratify the desires of the sinful nature." (Gal 5:16, NIV) It seemed to be saying that if I could live, or walk, by the Spirit that I would gain victory over lust. You would think it might say, "if you would stop living for your sinful desires, then you could walk by the Spirit," but this was a different equation: if you live by the Spirit, you will not live for sinful desires. That's what I wanted. Could it be that I could stop trying to control myself, and instead be changed from within?

Real and lasting transformation can take the place of struggle and defeat, but you have to change your orientation. Trying to control and defeat the power of sexual sin on your own is impossible. God has made a way for you to be changed and to have new desires, through what the Bible calls the *gospel*. The gospel is what transforms us from people who love and live for ourselves into those who love Christ and live to please him.

What is this gospel, this proclamation of good news? It is this: the love of Jesus Christ can set you free from the power of sin. Love conquers lust. You can experience freedom, lasting change, and hope for the future because of what Jesus Christ did on the cross on your behalf.

If your story is anything like mine, I hope that as you read this book you will find hope, and begin on a road to renewal, and joy.

How to Use This Book in a Group

The best way to read this book is with others. At the end of each chapter there are questions for discussion. You will have an opportunity to hear others' stories, share your own, and pray together. Even getting with one person to go over this book will be more helpful than being on your own, because you will be able to experience the freedom that comes from confession, and build deeper friendships that heal.

It will be difficult to study this guide with a mixed group of men and women. You need to be with people who can reveal personal, often painful details of their lives with each other. In addition, being in a mixed group can stifle sharing embarrassing details; those details can also be unnecessarily enticing when they come from a person of the opposite sex.

If you do use this book in a group, have each person read a couple of paragraphs out loud. It might seem better to have a leader, or someone more eloquent do all the readings, but the whole group should participate if possible. The role of the group leader is to keep things on track, and encourage participation.

At the end of the reading there are a number of discussion questions. Open these up to the group. Try to keep your answers personal. Saying "I know a guy who once did this and that" is anecdotal, not personal. You will benefit most from this material if you apply it to yourself first.

Every time you get together each member of the group should "get current." Discuss how your has week been (if you're meeting weekly.) The Bible tells us to "confess your sins to one another and pray for one another, that you may be healed. The prayer of a righteous person has great power as it is working." (James 5:16) The importance of this cannot be over-emphasized. One thing that every one agrees on in dealing with sexual sin is the importance of confession. Confession need not be sexually explicit; you can easily run the danger of triggering another person's desire with graphic descriptions. Rather, it should be a matter-of-fact accounting of success and failure.

It is important to pray when you get together for each member in the group. If you find that you are running out of time for prayer when you meet you should adjust your discussion time, or break the reading up into smaller units. Like confession, prayer is critical for acknowledging God's power and inviting him into your plan of recovery. In addition, make it a goal to pray for yourself and others in your group. As we saw above in the passage from James, "The prayer of a righteous person has great power." Don't underestimate that power.

Acknowledgements

This book could never have been written without the help of many people.

This material comes from a course that I developed for Xenos Christian Fellowship called *Sexual Integrity for Men*, as well as from personal counseling with men who have struggled with a variety of sexual problems. It comes from my own search for answers in God's word, as I confronted my own struggle with pornography. That search led me to many sources, and I owe an enormous debt of gratitude to those who helped me along the way. Many of these were men who courageously confronted and encouraged me. Others are writers, counselors, teachers and theologians whose work I have used to frame my own thinking on this subject. I am "standing on the shoulders of giants."

I want to thank my wife, Leslie, who has stood by me for 35 years, through thick and thin, through the worst of times as well as the best. Her support has been an amazing demonstration of the grace of God. In answer to the question that Solomon proposed in Proverbs 31:10, "An excellent wife, who can find?" – apparently, "I can".

I want to thank those who have spoken truth into my life, and who have been used by God to bring me back from the darkness – my son Colin, Tim Lipovsky, Chris Lang, Kerr Gibson, and Jon Rue. You guys were there for me with courage and love.

I want to thank those who have supported me in developing this material – Phil Franck, Mike Sullivan, Dennis McCallum, Gary Delashmutt, Ron Olah, and George Verwer. Thanks to go to Colin Gardner, and

Dr. Teresa Myers for early edits and suggestions. Teresa also gave me invaluable help with the discussion questions. A very special thanks go to Christine Walker, whose major editorial assistance throughout this project has made me a better writer, and whose prayers and encouragement mean so much.

I want to thank the guys in my Friday night men's study, who were the first guinea pigs for the text of the book – Mykhaylo, Vince, Ben, Josh, Jesse, Anthony, and Leon, as well as the hundreds of men who have taken the Sexual Integrity class. Their testimony of the power of the love of Christ over sin is a great attestation to his glory.

Special thanks go to the men and women whose testimonies are recorded in this book. Their stories are told anonymously, but their praise will come from God.

All praise goes to my Lord Jesus Christ, who brought me out of darkness into the excellence of his light.

ONE

THE PROBLEM WITH PORN

It always started innocently enough: I would be on my computer, checking email, surfing information or news sites, downloading music, or even writing up a Bible study. My children downstairs were asleep, and 15 feet away from me in my bedroom my wife and the German shepherd were alternately breathing and snoring. It was time. I would go to a search engine and begin typing in the words that would take me on a dark journey, one that had become second-nature and all too familiar. Soon, a parade of images of naked women would appear on my computer screen.

I would lose all track of time as this procession marched past my eyes. When it was over, I would close the program, and an immediate sense of shame would spread over me. "I can't believe I did that again," I would tell myself. A glance at the clock told me that it was 3 AM. Where had the time gone? I had to be at work at 8 o'clock! My thoughts would darken further as I thought about a Bible study I had to teach the next day – "God will never honor my teaching. I'm sure to fail."

Dread would wash over me as I slid carefully under the covers next to my sleeping wife; real sleep for me would be a long time coming, as I promised to do better next time.

If you've been involved with pornography, it's likely that there are elements of this story you can relate to. Could this be you? Do you consider yourself a committed Christian, and yet have a secret life that brings you shame? Maybe pornography is not really your thing; perhaps you find yourself returning to sexual fantasies and masturbation, going to strip clubs or massage parlors, or even prostitutes. Perhaps you are the kind of person who moves from one sexual relationship to another, living a life of flirtation, pursuit, and conquest. Whatever your problem with sex, the underlying causes are much the same.

What is common to all of us who are involved in sexual sin is the effect that it has on our lives. Sexual sin hurts us relationally: it darkens our relationship with God, our spouses, girlfriends, family, and friends. If you are involved in Christian ministry, the feelings of guilt haunt you every time you teach the Bible, or counsel someone about their problems, or try to share Christ with a friend. It's very hard to help others with issues in their lives when your own conscience is guilty. If you begin to devote more and more of your life to the pursuit of sexual pleasure, you can lose a job, a marriage, your children, your girlfriend, your ministry, and even end up in prison.

Before you say that none of that can happen to you, understand that every person whose life has been ruined by sexual sin probably said the same thing at one time. Sin is always deceiving (Hebrews 3:13).

There is no need to continue the cycle of sin, guilt, and shame. Hope and freedom are available to you right now by the power of God through Jesus Christ. God promises you: "He who began a good work in you will perfect it until the day of Christ Jesus" (Philippians 1:6). Throughout this book we will explore how God's truth renews our minds, and how living in community with others brings hope and freedom. You can be free of the power of sexual lust and enter fully into the joy of sex as God intended.

Sex is good, because the God who created sex is good. He created sex so that two people could experience a spiritual oneness and intimacy—a bond that is born in commitment, and sealed in delight. God created people in sexual purity, so that they would profoundly enjoy the bond between a man and woman.

In our rebellion against God, our sexuality has been deeply affected; we have fallen far from God's design. Today we are in a battle for our hearts, and the false gods of this world are being paraded before us in unprecedented array — a Vanity Fair to draw us away from the one true God, and his design for sex.

Before we enter into this battle, we should survey the battleground.

What Are We Up Against?

The apostle Paul tells us in Romans 1 that our rebellion against God has its deepest expression in sexual immorality. "Therefore God gave them up in the lusts of their hearts to impurity, to the dishonoring of their bodies among themselves, because they exchanged the truth about God for a lie and worshiped and served the creature rather than the Creator." (Romans 1:24-25) Because we decided to worship what God created rather than God, one of the most important aspects of being human became stained with lust. People began to look to anything but God for satisfaction because they had lost the knowledge of him, and sought only to know and please themselves. Sexual desire ran out of its bounds, and is running riot.

That impulse to put our sexual desires out of proportion stays with us, even as we become Christians and grow in our faith. Temptations abound. In our culture, sex has become an obsession of godlike proportions. We are surrounded by sexual images in every form of media. People speak frankly of sex in a way that would have been unheard of even 50 short years ago. Provocatively dressed people seem to be everywhere we go. As a culture, we have gone from thinking that sex is a normal part of life to believing that sex is the most important part of life.

Pornography is glamorized on television and in mainstream movies: we have television shows about women who pose in Playboy, girl-on-girl kissing no longer shocks us, and housewives exercise to "cardio striptease" videos. What you can see in lingerie ads in magazines or commercials is more like what you use to have to buy from behind the counter. This trend will continue as the line that had once been drawn on what constitutes obscenity will be redrawn over and over by our postmodern culture's moral confusion and obsessive view of sex. How Christians respond to this pornification of media will become important, especially as the lines between what is porn and what is just typical television programming become more blurred.

You are threatened by more than just our sex-obsessed culture. God's enemy, Satan, wants to demoralize and defeat you, taking you out of commission from any service or passion for God. As long as you are convinced that God could never love you because of what you've done, the devil is satisfied. If you are regularly involved in sexual sin, he doesn't have to do much else to achieve his end. Satan wants you off the battleground, and he doesn't care how he accomplishes this: the Tempter will entice you into sinning, and then the Accuser will condemn you for it afterwards.

So we're wounded, surrounded by temptation, and under the accusation and assault of a spiritual enemy. This is a tough battleground. It's no wonder that so many of us are wandering around somewhere between lust and shame. We can't stop thinking about sex, acting on our desires, and feeling terrible about it. We even foolishly think that if we could get enough sex, we would stop feeling bad.

The cycle of sin and defeat goes on and on, and we find ourselves feeling helpless and hopeless. If that isn't enough, the chemistry of our brains becomes a casualty in the battle—our brain fundamentally changes as we adapt to pornography's message.

Your Brain on Porn

Pornography affects your thinking like a disease that attacks an organ with no pain receptors. Others may be able to see the effects of this malady (if anyone can get close enough) but the one involved often can't see that they are being changed.

Pornography turns a man's mind inward, driving him to live in a self-centered world of sensual fantasy. Men become enraptured with themselves, unable to move away from self-love, as they stay glued to the video screen.

This in turn has an inevitable effect on your relationships. By using pornography you are divorcing sex from any relationship, and will begin to believe that there is no real connection between the two. As you do so over time, your ability to enter into relationships with women becomes inhibited. Pamela Paul is a journalist who interviewed dozens of men and women about the impact of pornography on their lives. In her book *Pornified* she says, "Because pornography involves looking at women but not interacting with them, it elevates the physical while ignoring or trivializing all other aspects of the woman."[1]

Pornography turns women into objects to be consumed. Like a bucket of fried chicken a woman is nothing more than breasts, legs, and thighs. "The porn star is a blank slate on which each observer can graft his own recipe for reciprocal lust and pleasure."[2] In porn a woman isn't a person and she doesn't have thoughts and feelings. Rather, she is a *commodity* to be consumed by men for their own pleasure. This is the antithesis of what God intended. When God created woman, the private beauty of her body was to be cherished, the gift of her sex protected. Pornography degrades and perverts what God has created.

1. Pamela Paul, *Pornified*, (New York, Henry Holt and Cie., 2005), 80
2. Ibid, 78

Proponents of pornography claim that it safely relieves sexual tension. This is not true. In fact, porn *creates* sexual tension, insecurity, and passivity. Men who look at porn know they don't measure up to the idealized images of men who perform with the women they are lusting after.

> "Pornography, with its mutual objectification and teenage mentality, can bring back the worst of adolescent fears about manhood (with its requirements for youthful vigor and boundless constitution). This mounting tension then leads the search for temporary relief – and a more intense drive toward more porn."[3]

Men who look at porn find less enjoyment in normal sex.

> "The 2004 Elle-MSNBC.com poll found that as a result of viewing online pornography, one in ten men said that he or his partner was bored with their sex routine; 17 percent said that viewing pornography made sex less arousing. One in ten admitted he had become more critical of his partner's body."[4]

Additionally, men can lose the ability to be aroused by their real-life partners, and even have trouble achieving orgasm during normal sex. They find themselves re-imagining scenes from the pornography they have seen in order to achieve climax, or have to masturbate to have an orgasm. Intercourse becomes boring, while oral, manual, and sometimes anal sex take center stage as the

---

3. Ibid, 82
4. Ibid, 91

preferred items on the sexual menu. Men who look at porn may ask their partners to act out scenes they have seen in pornography. If the partner refuses to engage in these behaviors when they find them objectionable or risky, these same men may go as far as to seek out prostitutes to perform things from their favorite movies. Pornography is having a decisive effect on driving the demand side of prostitution.[5]

Pornography damages more than just a couple's sexual health. It also leads to deception in relationships. Those men who get deeper into pornography have an essentially secret world, especially from their wives.

> "But while men consider trust crucial for a healthy relationship, they seem willing to flout that trust when it comes to pornography – deceiving their significant others into thinking they're either not looking at it at all or looking at it less frequently."[6]

Habitual pornography users deceive themselves as well. This shows itself in the series of promises and lies that they tell themselves. "This will be the last time," "The girls in these pictures aren't really naked," "My wife is sick right now, so we're not going to have sex anyway," "I'll do this as long as I'm single, but I can stop once I get married." The lies and rationalizations can go on endlessly as your attention is gently diverted away from your failure to be a real man, and turned towards a weak and flawed version of masculinity.

---

5. For more evidence on this topic, see http://captivedaughters. org/demand.htm

6. Paul, p. 99

The Death of Intimacy

We were made to experience intimacy, to enter deeply and fully into the world of another person. Sex is one form of intimacy, but there are others, such as the kind we can share with children, siblings, parents, or friends. Our need for intimacy is vital to us. Consider all the love songs that have been written: most of them aren't about having an orgasm, but rather about the desire for a deep kind of sharing. While there are lots of popular songs replete with sexual innuendo, most are about simple things like spending time together, wanting to be with the person, experiencing the loss of parting, or hoping to restore a broken relationship. Our music and art reflect our need for intimate relationships.

By contrast, pornography creates an experience of *false intimacy*, the illusion of a pain-free, safe substitute for real intimacy. Worse than that, it affects the mind of the person who uses it such that it erodes the ability to be intimate with others over time.

> "Pornography corrupts the ability to be intimate. It pulls consumers and producers in with the promise of intimacy, but fails to deliver the connection between two human beings."[7]

William Struthers has written a recent book on pornography's effect on the brain, called *Wired for Intimacy: How pornography hijacks the male brain*. Struthers' background is in neuroscience, and he explains how this corruption of intimacy works.

---

7. William M. Struthers, *Wired for Intimacy: How pornography hijacks the male brain*, (Downers Grove, IVP, 2009), 43

"Many men can spend hours looking at pornography… as they do, they are neurologically training themselves to respond to the type of images they view… As porn and fantasy take control of the mind, it becomes a dream theater that is transposed over the waking world. Every woman they come in contact with is objectified, undressed, and evaluated as a willing (or unwilling) mental sexual partner."[8]

How can you have intimacy with a woman when all women are reduced to nothing more than pieces of meat to be consumed at your discretion? Women who are not pretty enough are discarded; those who meet with your physical standards are sexualized without their consent. You may even think that these women desire you, as your fantasies overlay reality. Porn trains men who use it to see all women as ready and willing, but it depersonalizes them. They're not real people.

"When pornography is acted upon, sexual technique replaces sexual intimacy. In the absence of a meaningful relational context, nearly all of the elements of truly meaningful sexual intimacy are absent. Pornography teaches its students to focus on the physiology of sexual sensations and not on the relationships for which those sensations are intended."[9]

"Porn is a whispered promise. It promises more sex, better sex, endless sex, sex on demand, more

8. Ibid, 44-45
9. Ibib, 55

intense orgasms, experiences of transcendence."[10]

"When men realize that they have bought a lie and that it has failed to deliver on its promise of intimacy, they become imprisoned by shame. They intuitively know that they need true intimacy, but they are incapable of having it when they are in isolation from real relationships with real people."[11]

The picture is bleak. Pornography silently, insidiously destroys the thinking of men. Is porn costing you your life? Ultimately, it's not just costing you *your* life: there is significant human toll among those who make pornography.

The Price of Porn

"Porn was a horrible experience, having to stay in the same position while they re-did shots and having to re-do positions all the time. I wasn't allowed to wipe anything off my face or body until they were done. It was really gross and really degrading as a woman... I developed an eating disorder which I had to be hospitalized for several times. I think I am not able to have kids now because of all the physical problems I had. Sometimes I was pounded so hard I bled, my periods were always off key. I caught gonorrhea when I was 18 by another guy I was asked to have sex with on film without a rubber. I never caught anything from prostituting

---

10. Ibid, 69
11. Ibid, 57

but did from doing porn." – Kristenye Riddick, former porn actress[12]

Does her testimony make you uncomfortable? It should. However, many men today tend to see pornography as something that is fairly harmless. The arguments go like this:

- The people who make pornography are professionals, not victims.
- The actors are working voluntarily and are paid a lot of money for what they do.
- They seem to enjoy working in the industry. They say as much when we (increasingly) see them interviewed on television, or in magazine articles, or in their best selling autobiographies.
- Spokespeople for the industry, such as Ron Jeremy and Jenna Jameson, talk about the positive effects that porn has, like helping people get in touch with their sexuality, and using pornography as a form of safer sex.

The truth is that pornography degrades and dehumanizes women and glamorizes rape, torture, abuse, and slavery. It encourages child molestation, and is an important factor in driving the demand in international sex trafficking. While pornography is destroying relationships, it also destroys those who make it.

---

12. Quoted from www.thepinkcross.org

Pornography Objectifies Women

Shelly Lubben is a former porn actress who has been reaching out with the good news about Jesus Christ to sex and pornography workers. On her web site you can read the testimonies of many women who have been set free from the porn industry. In every case, they describe how they hated making porn, hated the men who abused them, and had to use drugs and alcohol just to get through a sex scene. Go to her site (www.thepinkcross.org) and read these testimonials – they will enlighten you as to what is really going on in the industry.

Elizabeth Rollings describes for us what it was like to make what has become a very popular genre, a 25-man sex scene.

> *"For two days I had to fast. I drank heavily one day prior before I did the movie. When I got on the set I felt really sick to my stomach. I wanted to turn around and run when I walked through the door and saw all the male porn stars and film crew standing there. I zoned out and wanted it to be over. I kept saying to myself, "this is going to be over in an hour. You can do it." I wanted to break down and cry but I hid behind my fake smile."*

> *"During the movie I mentally and emotionally checked out and felt like I died. I don't remember real well the pain and trauma I went through. After it ended, everybody wanted to take pictures with me and get my autograph. Here I am standing there with bodily fluids all over me and people wanted to take pictures with me. It was horrible. My body*

was sore the next couple of days and I wasn't right mentally for two weeks after that. I wasn't able to use the bathroom right either. My internal system was totally messed up."[13]

In order to inflict this kind of suffering, you would have to distance yourself from the humanity of a person. The same is true for those who watch and enjoy this kind of film. These women (and men) become objects of lust; they stop being people. We fool ourselves into believing that these sex workers enjoy what they are doing so that we can enjoy what we are doing while we watch their degradation.

Pornography Is a Significant Factor in Human Trafficking

Melissa Farley, a psychologist who has spent extensive time studying post-traumatic stress disorder among prostitutes, makes the following observations:

"When men use pornography, in that process they are trained as tricks. Pornography is men's rehearsal for prostitution."[14]

"In interviews with 854 women in prostitution in 9 countries, women and men in prostitution made it clear that pornography is integral to prostitution. In 9 countries, almost half (49 percent) told us that pornography was made of them while they

13. www.thepinkcross.org

14. Melissa Farley, "Renting an Organ for Ten Minutes: What Tricks Tell Us about Prostitution, Pornography, and Trafficking", *Pornography: Driving the Demand in International Sex Trafficking*, (Captive Daughters Media), 144-145

were in prostitution. Forty-seven percent of our respondents were upset by tricks' attempts to make them do what the tricks had previously seen in pornography." In another study "Eighty percent said that tricks showed them pornography in order to illustrate the specific sex acts that they wanted performed."[15]

Several years ago, noted feminist and journalist Gloria Steinem said,

"Pornography is a marketing device for sex trafficking: It normalizes degradation and violence as acceptable and even inevitable parts of sex, and uses the bodies of real women and children as objects. The difference between pornography and erotica is clear in the roots of the words themselves — *porne* means female slaves, *eros* means love — so pornography, like rape, is about violence and domination, not sex. Millions of lives depend on our ability to separate pornography from erotica, and to disentangle violence from sexuality."[16]

There are as many as two million sex slaves in the world, and pornography is a significant factor in creating demand for prostitutes. According to Dr. Farley, tricks are trained with pornography. Men who look at pornography gain a taste for things they cannot (and often should never) find at home. Instead, they can rent what they are looking for. As Douglas Weiss, executive

15. Ibid, 145
16. Gloria Steinem, *Erotica and Pornography: A Clear and Present Difference*. Ms. Magazine. November 1978, p. 53

director of Heart to Heart Counseling Center in Colorado Springs told an interviewer, "If a guy masturbates to something it would take a prostitute to do, he's more likely to find one."[17]

If half of the prostitutes interviewed have had pornography made of them, and you have spent any significant amount of time looking at Internet pornography, especially of so-called "amateurs", odds are that you have watched a prostitute being abused against her will. Odds are that you've watched someone underage suffering that same abuse. Though you may not have known it, you have probably been a consumer of child pornography. This degradation of a child has its origin in hell, and you have probably unwittingly found enjoyment in it.

Knowing this, can you look at what you do on your computer the same way again?

The Bible's Views on the Effects of Pornography

While it might be hard to imagine that its authors had no concept of the hyper-sexualized world of the 21st century, the damaging effects of sexual sin are not unknown to the Bible. The men who wrote the Bible saw the negative effects of sexual sin in their own cultures, which in many ways were as decadent as our own. Their warnings often point to how a man's life could be destroyed by an obsession with sex:

> "Flee from sexual immorality. Every other sin
> a person commits is outside the body, but the

---

17. quoted by John W. Kennedy, *Help for the Sexually Desperate*, Christianity Today, March 2008

sexually immoral person sins against his own body."
(1 Corinthians 6:18)

"Can a man carry fire next to his chest and his
clothes not be burned? Or can one walk on hot
coals and his feet not be scorched? So is he who
goes in to his neighbor's wife; none who touches
her will go unpunished." (Proverbs 6:27–29)

"With much seductive speech she persuades him;
with her smooth talk she compels him. All at once
he follows her, as an ox goes to the slaughter, or as
a stag is caught fast till an arrow pierces its liver; as
a bird rushes into a snare; he does not know that it
will cost him his life." (Proverbs 7:21–23)

Pursuing sexual sin leads our hearts away from God,
the one true source of all life and joy. Pain and suffering
will always be the result. You can't spend hours each week
looking at pornography without being affected by it.

So What Do We Do?

Pornography isn't harmless entertainment; it devas-
tates both its consumers and producers. Lives are ruined,
relationships are undermined, and genuine sexual satisfaction becomes more and more elusive. Our culture's
dream of unbounded sexual pleasure has turned into a
nightmare of shattered dreams.

To be free you must turn your back on porn. But you
can't turn away from one thing with nowhere else to go.
Instead, you must turn towards something, or someone.
In truth, there is only One whom you can turn to that
can defeat the power of lust in your life and make you

whole again. It is the One who took the penalty for your wrongdoing upon himself to bring you into a relationship with God. That One is Jesus Christ. He lived a perfect life, died on a cross so that he could bear your sin, and conquered death by his resurrection. As a result you can be completely accepted by God based on what Jesus has done.

If you do not consider yourself a Christian, I strongly encourage you to examine the claims of Jesus and ask God to show you whether or not they are true. No matter what you have done or how you've lived your life, his offer of salvation and freedom is there for the asking. You'll learn more about it in the pages that follow, and I invite you to join me in the journey towards real freedom.

If you are a Christian, you already know about salvation through Jesus Christ. Yet, how well have you understood the grace of God? Have you been fully convinced that you are unable to please God on your own merits? Are you trying (and failing) to be a good enough Christian for God to accept you? Do you see the gospel, the good news of salvation through Christ, as something that only applies to someone who is not a Christian?

Throughout this book we will unravel the mystery of how the love of Christ overcomes sin, how the truth of God's word renews our minds, and how living with others in community sets us free to experience joy in relating. The goal of this book is not just to get you to stop doing something, but to start living life to its fullest.

For group discussion

Have each person give the group a brief personal history of their involvement with pornography or sexual sin. How did you get involved? Where are you now? Discuss the effect that your involvement in sexual sin has had on your life and relationships.

In what ways have you felt ashamed, defeated, or hopeless? In what ways have you justified your actions to yourself or others?

Are you optimistic about what God can do in your life right now? What are your goals are for the future?

Pray for each member in your group. Pray in hope, knowing that he who is in you is greater than he who is in the world, and in faith that God wants to restore you.

Two

My Problem with Porn

Maybe you've thought that pornography is a small sin, especially in comparison to adultery or murder. You may have even told yourself that you are avoiding more serious sexual sins by using pornography. When you're involved in porn there is a sense of unreality that blinds you to its effects, that is, until something serious happens. Getting discovered by your spouse, or getting caught looking at porn at work and losing your job are serious reality checks. In most cases, there is a wake up call before anyone will decide to do something about a habit of pornography. My own story of discovery goes something like this:

> *It was a muggy June night in central Ohio, just prior to going on a vacation with my wife for our anniversary, and some of the guys I was leading a home Bible study with invited me over for a talk. When I got to my friends house I immediately sensed an air of sobriety: something was wrong here. The four of us sat in the back yard and one of them started right in. "Brian, we think you have a problem, and we want to ask you. Are you using pornography?" I immediately felt shame, anger, panic, and wonder. How did they know? For years I had steadily become more and more embroiled in the dark late night world of Internet porn, and somehow it was apparent. I also felt relief, because*

I had been hiding this problem from them, and now that the truth was out, I could finally stop hiding. They probed with their questioning: how often? What kind of material? At first I minimized and dodged, but they were persistent, and I knew their concern was genuine.

I promised that I would stop. I promised that I would tell my wife about it. I quit for a while, and then I resumed. At first, it was a slow return, just a peek here and there at some suggestive images, just an occasional session in front of the computer. I didn't want to tell anyone because they would worry that I was hooked, addicted. I decided that since I wasn't progressing to more serious forms of sexual behavior such as strip clubs, massage parlors, and prostitutes, I couldn't really be addicted. After all, I was looking at the same kind of soft-core material I had looked at when I was a boy stealing my dad's Playboys. After all, I had what I thought was a healthy sexual relationship with my wife. After all, I was doing just fine.

I had my position to consider: I was a leader in the church; people looked up to me. I could lose all of that if I admitted that I had a porn problem. So I continued in silence, and once again I was back to spending hours each week, and sometimes each day, looking at pictures on my computer. After a while the load of guilt and sense of conviction were so great that I went to the leaders in my church and confessed that I had continued using

*porn and lying to them. I had become enslaved to
pornography.*

One of the problems men have with pornography
is that they don't see it as a serious issue. After all, it's
just you and your computer and your body. Secular psychologists almost universally teach that masturbation
and fantasy are normal expressions of our sexuality, so
what's the big deal?

Sexual lust is a sin, and God takes all sin seriously. Sin
caused a separation between God and us (Isaiah 59:1-2).
That separation is so total that only through sending his
Son to pay the full penalty for sin could God accept us
into a relationship (1 John 4:9-10). Without salvation
through Christ, the payment for sin is eternal destruction
(1 Corinthians 15:22, 2 Thessalonians 1:9).

For those of us who know Christ, sin breaks our experience of fellowship with God (1 John 1:6). It's *not* just
you and your body; God is involved, and you are will-
fully deciding to break your fellowship with him. This
is not just a violation of a set of rules or a moral code:
the offence against God is personal (Psalm 51:4). To
minimize and *tolerate* sin is to decide to move away from
God. Pornography affects your relationships with other
people too. In fact, using porn is *anti-relational*. Porn
impairs your ability to have relationships with others
by providing a substitute for the feelings that belong in
human relationships without requiring you to invest in
the lives of others or risk relational pain.

Over time you will experience an increasing distance
between yourself and others when you have a part of
your life that you aren't sharing with anyone. Because

you want to keep up appearances you'll hide from those around you. The deterioration of your relationships will cause you pain, which will drive you back into a convenient means of anesthesia – more porn. You will never be satisfied while you try to slake your thirst for meaningful relationships with the salt water of counterfeit relating with two-dimensional objects of desire.

Many Christians who look at porn are also involved in ministry. We've all seen the scandals surrounding men in ministry who have fallen prey to the lure of sex. They bring shame to their families, their churches, and to the cause of Christ. Any form of sexual sin will significantly reduce or altogether impede your effectiveness. It will also deaden the enjoyment of your service to God. While God can still use you when you are in sin, just as he can when you are proud or angry, the feelings of guilt and shame will hound you every time you try to minister to others. You'll feel like a hypocrite whenever you advise someone about his or her own problems. Every Bible teaching you hear will somehow be about you and your silence.

If you keep saying no to God's gentle pressure, eventually your ability to minister to others will decline completely. Then the worst thing that could happen might become true of you: you will lose your dream of serving God with your life. God might even leave you to yourself. What a tragedy! If you are in a public position and get discovered, the damage that can be done to the name of Christ can be profound.

Is Pornography Addictive?

The term "pornography addiction" has emerged recently. Can you be addicted to porn like you can to heroin? Is it important or even helpful to call yourself an addict? The National Council on Sexual Addiction and Compulsivity has defined sexual addiction as "engaging in persistent and escalating patterns of sexual behavior acted out despite increasing negative consequences to self and others."[1] Negative consequences can be things such as deteriorating relationships, or a sense of isolation from others. It can be as seemingly innocuous as missing a kid's soccer game because you stayed home to look at porn, or as bad as getting fired from a job for violating their Internet policy. When you miss these wake-up calls, you've lost control.

Have you promised to stop looking at pornography and were unable to do so? Then, for you it is a serious problem and could be called an addiction. This idea is not foreign to the Scriptures: the Bible teaches that sin that is repeated is enslaving (Proverbs 5:22; John 8:34; Hebrews 12:1). Paul says in his letter to the Romans, "When you offer yourselves to someone to obey him as slaves, you are slaves to the one whom you obey—whether you are slaves to sin, which leads to death, or to obedience, which leads to righteousness." (Romans 6:16)

The term "voluntary slavery" might be more accurate — we choose to offer ourselves to lust, so it's voluntary, but find ourselves in the grip of sin, enslaved to it. One

---

1. The National Council on Sexual Addiction and Compulsivity - www.ncsac.org and www.sash.net

of the best definitions of addiction I've seen comes from
Ed Welch, of the Christian Counseling and Education
Foundation (CCEF):

> "Addiction is bondage to the rule of a substance,
> activity, or state of mind, which then becomes the
> center of life, defending itself from the truth so
> that even bad consequences don't bring repentance,
> and leading to further estrangement from God."[2]

Addiction to Internet pornography is aided by what
is called the "triple-A threat" — *accessibility*, *anonymity*,
and *affordability*. First, Internet pornography is perhaps
the most accessible commodity on the Internet. With
around half a billion pages, it's easier to find porn on the
Web than a good deal on a set of tires.

Secondly, surfing for porn gives you the illusion that
you are alone, and the only person involved. When you're
on your computer late at night while your wife is sleeping, or your roommates are out of the house, no one can
see you. Your browser history and cache can be cleared,
downloaded files can be deleted, and you think you've
gotten away with it.

Third, it is affordable: magazines and movies cost
money, but there are billions of free pornographic images
and movies available on the Internet. This makes it especially convenient for children and college students to
get access to material they might not otherwise be able
to pay for.

These three traits create the perfect medium for sin
to thrive. In the fantasy world of pornography, anything

---

2. Ed Welch, *Addictions: A Banquet in the Grave*, (Phillipsburg, Puritan and Reformed Publishing, 2001), 35

we desire is available to us without cost, without responsibility or circumstance, and without the oversight of any moral authority. In our minds we become like petty gods where nothing is denied our vanity and lust. That's addicting.

How did I get this way?

If you are hooked on pornography, you may have asked yourself, "How did I get this way?" When you realize that you have a problem it is natural to start looking in your past for background causes for addictive behavior. Was I abused sexually as a child? Is there something about my upbringing that caused this tendency? Do I have an "addictive" personality? While these are legitimate questions, the bottom line is that we are all sinners, though in different ways. If you have a problem with pornography, fantasy, and masturbation, your sexuality is one area where your sin issues take center stage.

Sin is something that is familiar to us, and yet we can find it mysterious at the same time. We have been disobeying God our whole lives, but we say things like, "how did that happen?" or "I can't believe I did that!" When you become angry with another driver on the freeway you don't really wonder *why* it happened again - some sins you take for granted. There is a different quality to the realization that you have become hooked on pornography. It seems so pathological, downright creepy even. So how does it happen?

In 1992, just one year before the introduction of the first graphical web browser, it was fairly easy to predict the background of a person who was a sexual addict. At that time, Patrick Carnes, a leading researcher in the area of sexual addiction, said:

> "Research has found that sex addicts often come from dysfunctional families and are more likely than non-sex addicts to have been abused. One study found that 82 percent of sex addicts reported being sexually abused as children. Sex addicts often describe their parents as rigid, distant and uncaring. These families, including the addicts themselves, are more likely to be substance abusers. One study found that 80 percent of recovering sex addicts report some type of addiction in their families of origin."[3]

By 2001, less than ten years later, the World Wide Web was a household word, boasting around 500 million users. Pornography sites, news feeds, and sexual chat rooms were springing up at an exponential rate. At that time, having heard the stories of many who had become addicted to sex on the Internet, Dr. Carnes had the following observations:

> "We find that there is no way to predict who will have a problem with cybersex.[4] Those who do come from a broad range of ethnic, social, and economic backgrounds. They can be people who've had trouble with sex before and people for whom it's never been a problem. They may be people

3. Patrick Carnes, Ph.D., *Out of the Shadows*, (Center City, Hazelden, 1992)

4. This is a term that Carnes uses to refer to sexual content on the Internet, as well as sexual activity, such as sexually oriented chat rooms.

with healthy or unhealthy coping responses. This is one of the unique aspects of cybersex. In other sexual problems, it's possible to detect patterns or common points — such as childhood sexual or emotional abuse or a familial history of addictive disorders, for example — among the people who are struggling. Not so with cybersex."[5]

There is *something new* about Internet pornography that had not been previously witnessed by counselors and researchers in sexual addiction. Internet porn seems to have the power to rule those who use it, regardless of their background. This is particularly true of younger men and boys, whose sexual identity and interests are still forming.

Pornography taps in to our natural self-centeredness. The women in porn are idealized: always ready, always willing, always admiring. They don't say no to you. You are always good looking enough, you don't have to maintain a standard of hygiene, or work at a relationship in order to experience their bodies (at least with your eyes and in your mind). The fantasy of porn feeds the ego that wants to be the center of the universe.

There is great danger with Internet pornography. With the vast array of options available to you, you are in complete control of the content and your arousal, you are disassociated from relationships, you are having it your way, and you can use it in the way that most depersonalizes the experience. Imagine the power of a drug where you can completely control the effects! Worse yet,

5. Patrick Carnes, *In the Shadows of the Net*, (Center City, Hazelden, 2001), 66

you may develop a taste for perversions that you never would have dreamed of. As Dr. Carnes observed,

> "Most of us have a part of our sexuality that lies unacknowledged, unexplored, and without a voice, and the Internet offers a way to explore that sexuality."[6]

You may have significant factors in your upbringing and sexual history that bear on your dependence on pornography, and you may not. No matter how you got to this point, the result is the same: you return again and again to the things that bring you shame. You keep coming back to the promise that porn offers, one of satisfaction and fulfillment, a momentary experience of transcendence, only to be robbed again of those very things you are seeking. It's a vicious cycle of false promises, and disappointment. This cycle is familiar to the teaching of the Bible, and it's called idolatry.

The Idol Factory

Most people think of *idolatry* as the worship of a statue or icon meant to represent some deity. The Biblical definition is broader than that: idolatry applies to anything that you have in your life that is a substitute for God. When your job is more important to you than God, it becomes an idol. When your family or a relationship becomes more important to you than God, they become idols. Sometimes it's just the approval of others that enslaves us. What makes something an idol for you is that you're looking to that thing, whatever it is, to give

---

6. Ibid, p. 60

life meaning, to validate you as a person. An idol is often something you feel you can't live without. If it were to be taken away, you would respond in anger, fear or grief.

Most idols are good things that have been expanded into ultimate things. The thing that has become an idol in your life might be very good, such as a relationship with a girl. Being in love is a good thing. When she breaks it off with you, and you're shattered and depressed and don't feel like living any more, that relationship is an idol. Loving your children is good, but when they don't turn out the way you wanted them to, and you're so angry that you can't stand to be with them, your children have become an idol. Idols take on a magnitude of meaning that is out of proportion with what they are or offer to you.

According to the Bible, idolatry is a fundamental problem of mankind. In the book of Deuteronomy the Lord gave what Jesus later called "The Great Commandment." The call is to "love God with all your heart, soul, and strength." This is contrasted with a warning against idolatry. "You shall not go after other gods, the gods of the peoples who are around you." (Deuteronomy 6:5, 14) From the golden calf in Exodus, throughout the history of God's people recorded in the books of Judges, Samuel, Kings, the prophets, and Psalms, idolatry was the snare that God's people fell into time and time again.

Sex and idolatry often go hand in hand. Sex was a large part of idol worship in ancient cultures. It was prominent in most of the forms of idolatry that Israel was drawn into, such as the worship of Baal and Ashtoreth. Ritual sex and cultic prostitution were an integral part of idol worship for both men and women.

"They sacrifice on the tops of the mountains and burn offerings on the hills, under oak, poplar, and terebinth, because their shade is good. Therefore your daughters play the whore, and your brides commit adultery." (Hosea 4:13)

Sex is one of God's greatest gifts, a gift that brings two people together in the closest of intimacies. God created man and woman to experience a special kind of unity realized through pleasure. It's no wonder that people have been preoccupied with sex from the beginning – the best gifts make the most powerful idols. In the first chapter of Romans, Paul gives us some insight into this connection with idolatry and sex. First, he says:

"For although they knew God, they did not honor him as God or give thanks to him, but they became futile in their thinking, and their foolish hearts were darkened. Claiming to be wise, they became fools, and exchanged the glory of the immortal God for images resembling mortal man and birds and animals and creeping things." (Rom 1:21-23)

Here then is the essence of idolatry: man has decided to throw off God's loving leadership, refusing to honor Him as the one deserving of our worship. Instead, he turns to the creation that God made to find meaning and fulfillment. Man chose to worship the gift rather than the Giver. As a result, man turned to one of God's greatest gifts—sex—and made it an idol. "Therefore God gave them up in the lusts of their hearts to impurity, to the dishonoring of their bodies among themselves, because they exchanged the truth about God for a lie and worshiped and served the creature rather than the Creator, who is blessed forever!" (Rom 1:24-25)

If sex is an idol for us, we turn from God as the one who provides us meaning and turn to sensuality to derive our meaning, validation, and fulfillment. Ironically, we won't find any of those things in sex. The free-love generation of the sixties is today characterized by unprecedented divorce and broken relationships. Younger generations seem to be unsatisfied with all of the sex they are having.[7]

We foolishly believe that if we can just get the formula right everything will be great. Instead, disappointment lurks around every corner. In the midst of all of this pursuit of sexual fulfillment, the Bible reminds us that idols always disappoint; they can never fulfill us the way God can.

The prophet Isaiah mocks the futility of those who think their idols can fulfill them but he does so with a sense of the tragedy. Describing someone who has cut wood for his fire as well as to fashion an idol, he says:

> "All who fashion idols are nothing, and the things they delight in do not profit. Their witnesses neither see nor know, that they may be put to shame. Who fashions a god or casts an idol that is profitable for nothing? … He cuts down cedars, or he chooses a cypress tree or an oak and lets it grow strong among the trees of the forest. He plants a cedar and the rain nourishes it. Then it becomes

---

7. For a much fuller examination of the dissatisfaction of the "hookup" culture, see Donna Freitas, *Sex and the Soul: juggling sexuality, spirituality, romance, and religion on America's college campuses* (New York, Oxford University Press, 2008)

fuel for a man. He takes a part of it and warms himself; he kindles a fire and bakes bread. Also he makes a god and worships it; he makes it an idol and falls down before it. Half of it he burns in the fire. Over the half he eats meat; he roasts it and is satisfied. Also he warms himself and says, "Aha, I am warm, I have seen the fire!" And the rest of it he makes into a god, his idol, and falls down to it and worships it. He prays to it and says, "Deliver me, for you are my god!" They know not, nor do they discern, for he has shut their eyes, so that they cannot see, and their hearts, so that they cannot understand. No one considers, nor is there knowledge or discernment to say, "Half of it I burned in the fire; I also baked bread on its coals; I roasted meat and have eaten. And shall I make the rest of it an abomination? Shall I fall down before a block of wood?" He feeds on ashes; a deluded heart has led him astray, and he cannot deliver himself or say, "Is there not a lie in my right hand?" (Isaiah 44:9-20)

Do you read a passage like this and think, "Oh, those silly ancient peoples and their primitive ways!" You aren't all that different. You make an idol out of power and control when you demand that life *must* go your way. You make an idol of the approval of others when you desperately look for acclaim and affirmation. You make an idol of sex when you are ruled by your love of pleasure, using it as a false savior from the pains and frustrations of life. Your "block of wood" just happens to be made of metal and plastic and glass, and costs a lot more than a log. Like those Isaiah was addressing, your heart has been deluded. You may still be at that place where the lie you've been living is hard to perceive. Is there a lie in your right hand?

The Old and New Testaments use different words for this problem of seeking after idols. The Old Testament uses "idolatry" almost exclusively to describe the things that steal our hearts away from God. In the New Testament that word would be "desires" (*epithumia* in Greek). This word is translated as lust, craving, desire, longing, or coveting in our English Bibles. It carries the sense that Calvin intended when he said,

> "The human heart is a factory of idols... every one of us is, from his mother's womb, expert in inventing idols... The evil in our desire typically does not lie in what we want, but that we want it too much."[8]

This is an "over-desire", a desire out of proportion. It's a desire that consumes us, pulling us away from relationships, responsibilities, and God.

Our desire for sex is natural, but when it consumes us, it begins to master us. We start putting that desire at the forefront of our lives. Since idols can never fulfill us they leave us disappointed and empty. As your search for happiness through sex disappoints, you may crave more, but it's just a block of wood, and it can never give you what only God can give.

Of course, idols always deliver *something*; pornography and masturbation deliver strong feelings of pleasure and excitement. The problem is that it's never enough. You always sense that you need more, and you foolishly

---

8. John Calvin, Institutes I, xi, 8

believe that *more* will satisfy you. The person caught up in porn never seems to realize that they're not really getting what they seek.

Peter talks about the person who is "so nearsighted that he is blind, having forgotten that he was cleansed from his former sins." (2 Peter 1:9). That perfectly describes the person who has traded God for sinful pleasure – he forgets who he is, and the one who made him that way.

Sin blinds us to its effect on our lives by blinding us to the truth. We forget who we really are in our perfect, redeemed standing before God. We revert to seeing ourselves as just men. Yet, we are meant to see ourselves differently. Look at how Peter portrays those who have been rescued from the dark folly of idolatry into a relationship with God:

> "But you are a chosen race, a royal priesthood, a holy nation, a people for his own possession, that you may proclaim the excellencies of him who called you out of darkness into his marvelous light. Once you were not a people, but now you are God's people; once you had not received mercy, but now you have received mercy." (1 Peter 2:9-10)

If you are a Christian, you have a new identity in Christ and you have a mission. You are called to proclaim the excellence of the One who showed you mercy, glorifying God with your life as one redeemed from darkness. This will satisfy your deepest longings in a way that nothing else can. Sex won't give you ultimate meaning and fulfillment. God promises that he is the one who will give to you as only he can, as you follow him.

So Now What?

So is sexual desire wrong? Is that our problem? Do we need to become non-sexual people in order to follow Christ? Not at all—rather than putting sex at the center of our lives, we need to put it in its proper place and put God back in his. Voluntary slavery to pornography is a *worship disorder*, and the solution is going to require replacing what we've been worshipping.

Freedom from sin begins with your relationship with God. Learning to love God more than sin is at the heart of real recovery. As you experience his love for you through the mercy shown you at the cross of Jesus Christ, the logical response is to worship him. All of the blessings of salvation, like those we listed from 1 Peter, are based on what Christ has done for us. Counselor David Powlison puts it this way:

> "The Gospel is better than unconditional love. The Gospel says, "God accepts you just as Christ is. God has 'contraconditional' love for you." Christ bears the curse you deserve. Christ is fully pleasing to the Father and gives you His own perfect goodness. Christ reigns in power, making you the Father's child and coming close to you to begin to change what is unacceptable to God about you. God never accepts me "as I am." He accepts me "as I am in Jesus Christ." The center of gravity is different. The true Gospel does not allow God's love to be sucked into the vortex of the soul's lust for acceptability and worth in and of itself. Rather, it radically decenters people—what the Bible calls

"fear of the Lord" and "faith"—to look outside themselves."[9]

We need to take a stand! There is a battle going on for your heart. Will you face the day ready to fight? Or will you give in to fear and lust? Satan has many weapons against the church. Is this the one he has chosen to use against you? You will need the cleansing power of God's grace to wash away the feelings of guilt and shame over how you have sinned, but you also need to be strong! Your Lord calls you into battle. Will you let our enemy take you down in the barracks, when victory is at hand on the battlefield? This life is short, yet it has eternal significance! The time for action is now!

Maybe once you had a dream of serving God with your whole life, but your ensnarement in lust has made that seem almost laughable. One of the greatest lies of Satan is to suggest that, because we've strayed from the Lord, he would never have us back, never call us again into battle. Satan uses the guilt of what we've done to strip us of our dream of radical commitment to Christ. John Piper, speaking at the Passion07 conference, said:

"The great tragedy is not mainly masturbation or fornication or acting like a peeping Tom (or curious Cathy) on the Internet. The tragedy is that Satan uses the guilt of these failures to strip you of every radical dream you ever had, or might have, and in its place give you a happy, safe, secure, American life of superficial pleasures until you die in your

9. David Powlison, "Idols of the Heart and 'Vanity Fair'", *The Journal of Biblical Counseling*, 13:2, Winter 1995, 49.

lakeside rocking chair, wrinkled and useless, leaving a big fat inheritance to your middle-aged children to confirm them in their worldliness."[10]

Does that last description sound like one of the worst things that could happen to you? Maybe you're still hearing the voice of the Lord, calling you back into a life of meaningful service to him. It's not too late!

Peter's failure in his denial of Christ during his trial was substantial, and after Jesus' resurrection, the Lord asked him "Do you love me?" When Peter said that he did, Jesus' next words were, "Feed my sheep." Along with forgiving Peter his terrible betrayal, Jesus called him out of himself into deeper commitment to those around him. He was also revealing to Peter that his repentance would affect more than just himself. This will be true for you as well.

There was a time when I thought there was no hope for me. I believed I would be mastered by my obsession with porn for the rest of my life. I had almost given up on God's call to settle for that life of "superficial pleasures" that John Piper was talking about. People caught up in sin are hopeless, because they think they're helpless. That was definitely true of me at that time of my life. I almost succumbed to that safe, secure, worthless life that Satan was offering me, but the song of Jesus in my heart would not be quieted.

Whether there is hope for you is not really dependent on you. We have only one hope, and that is the cross of

---

10. John Piper, "How to Deal with the Guilt of Sexual Failure for the Glory of Christ and His Global Cause," Jan. 4, 2007. The text and recording of this talk can be found at http://desiringgod.org.

Jesus Christ (Gal. 6:14). God is the one who will see you
to the end of your sojourn here on earth. In Psalm 23:3
David says of his Shepherd: "He guides me in the paths
of righteousness for his names sake." This is a reference
to God's covenant faithfulness — He *will be* faithful to
you for the sake of his own reputation, not because you
are faithful. Paul writes in 2 Tim 2:13, "if we are faithless, he remains faithful — for he cannot deny himself."

God remains faithful to us, not because we deserve it,
but because to do otherwise would be to deny his faithfulness to his people, and thus deny his own character.
The same God who has fulfilled his promise to redeem
us through his Son has promised to bring you into his
eternal kingdom in perfection. He will do it. The question for you is: Do you believe it? If so, will you live in
accordance with the hope that you have? Listen to the
words of Christ:

> "The thief comes only to steal and kill and destroy.
> I came that they may have life and have it abun-
> dantly. . . My sheep hear my voice, and I know
> them, and they follow me. I give them eternal life,
> and they will never perish, and no one will snatch
> them out of my hand. My Father, who has given
> them to me, is greater than all, and no one is able
> to snatch them out of the Father's hand. I and the
> Father are one." (John 10:10, 27-30)

Will you believe that Jesus is able to keep you? The
Good Shepherd keeps his covenant promise for his name's
sake. He made a promise to see you through, and he's
going to keep it. This is GOOD NEWS! Are you ready
to get started? Take a moment now to talk to God in

your heart. Commit your life to him, thanking him for his mercy. Make a decision right now that you're going to start seeking the will of God in your life, and turning aside from pornography. Make a commitment to him in your heart to remove all traces of pornography from your house and your computer. Decide now — don't hesitate. Then, follow it up with committing to following his plan for your life. God will graciously receive you as his adopted son; he won't forsake you or disappoint you. He will not let you down. He loves you that much.

For Group Discussion

Many people argue that pornography use isn't a big deal. What reasoning have you heard for why pornography isn't harmful? Which of these arguments do you (or have you) found at least somewhat convincing? What kind of rationalizations have you used to excuse your behavior?

Have you ever thought of pornography as an idol, a God-replacement? What did that look like for you — in other words, how did you use pornography to fulfill you in ways that only God was meant to? Were you disappointed in the long-term results?

In what ways have you experienced the cycle of expectation and disappointment talked about in the section on idolatry?

How have you experienced Satan's accusations about your ability to serve God because of your problem with sexual sin? Do you think it is possible to live a life of radical service if you've struggled in this area? Why or why not?

Pray for each member in your group. Pray that God would show you how to set aside the idols of your heart by increasing your understanding and knowledge of him and his grace.

Three

The False Solution

By now, you may be convinced that pornography is a serious problem. Let's assume that you've decided to do something about it. It's right at this point that you may become your own worst enemy. Here's a testimony from a man in my Sexual Integrity for Men class:

> *"I reached a point in my life where I realized I needed to stop, and start being real with God about my desires for pornography. I knew that I could look at porn any time I wanted to, but began wondering why I did it. Did it make me a more loving person? Does it give joy to the people in my life? Does it show me the majesty of my Savior?*
>
> *Having a filter on my computer was more like a sign that said "No Fishing from the Bridge" — just a reminder of what you can't have. I had no confidence that there was something more magical and awesome in loving my wife. If I ask Christ whether it's OK to look at porn, he is silent, but when I say, "Help me to love my wife!" he answers. That silence is not his approval; he's waiting for me to realize that he loves me, and has so much more for me than porn could ever offer."*

Going to Law School

Though we acknowledge God in our life, we usually try to deal with problems in our own strength. We believe that we have to find the power to stop sexual sin within ourselves, before involving God. We all tend to approach God on the basis of our performance, of "how we're doing." This is what the Bible calls our tendency to live "according to Law." What does it mean to live according to Law? It means that we expect God to be angry with us when we sin, and to be pleased with us when we do right. "If I stay away from pornography, God will be happy with me." A performance-based approach to God is deadly to your walk with Him.

This inherent legalism also ties in with what's called the addictive cycle. There are four stages to the cycle of sexual addiction:

Stage 1 - Preoccupation

You find your mind filled with sexual images and fantasies. Lustful thoughts overlay your normal thinking as you go about your everyday business. This preoccupation produces a trance-like state, and you begin an obsessive search for stimulation. As you do, the rational mind is set aside, and lust starts to replace the function of the thinking brain. Setting your conscience aside is important in this stage, because otherwise you might stop and think what it is that you're doing. This phase of the cycle is where the Christian's primary battle lies; once later stages have been entered, it's hard to stop. The war for your mind has begun. "Beloved, I urge you as sojourners and exiles to abstain from the passions of the flesh, which wage war against your soul." (1 Peter 2:11; see also 2 Corinthians 10:5)

Stage 2 – Ritualization

During this next phase you begin to plan how you're going to act out. At this point, you begin to shift over to autopilot. Psychologists refer to this as depersonalization—that feeling that you're watching yourself act, a sense that you have no control over the situation or your actions. This state intensifies preoccupation. If the thinking brain is engaged at all, it is more than likely making excuses and rationalizing the behavior to come. Addicts of all kinds have rituals (circling in your car near your favorite bar, or where you go to score drugs). For you it may be getting your environment secure, such as closing the blinds or the door, or it may be enhancing the preoccupation phase by surfing the web for "safe" but arousing images, such as browsing Facebook or Myspace profiles, going to fashion sites or photo blogs. You may use alcohol or drugs to lower your resistance to what is coming next. Though you may tell yourself that there is "really nothing wrong with this," it is all part of a plan.

Stage 3 – Sexual Compulsivity

You act out in whatever form your desire takes: looking at pornography, masturbating, etc. You complete what was planned. At this point there are two things that happen: intense pleasure releases the tension that has built up, perhaps over many hours from the first stage, and then almost immediately you move on to the next stage.

Stage 4 – Shame and Despair

Your thinking brain becomes re-engaged, and you realize that you've done it again; you've violated your conscience. You said you wouldn't do that again, and you did it anyway.

For the Christian, or any person with a religiously informed conscience, a voice inside of you appends the character and commands of God to your shame. "I should know better than this! I'm a Christian!" There is really nothing wrong with this thinking per se — you do know better — but what seems to happen so many times is that we resolve to deal with this problem on our own power. We vow to stop, or to do better next time. We're right that the action belongs to us, but we wrongly think that the power must also flow from us.

Remember that this is a cycle, so when these feelings of shame and worthlessness hit, most addicts start the cycle over again. The pain they feel is too much to handle, and so relief is sought in the form of fantasy and lust. The cycle begins again.

Legalists at heart

We are all legalists at heart, even those of us with completely non-religious upbringing. I came out of the 60's hippie culture of sex, drugs, and rock and roll, but when I became a Christian in 1974, I immediately began to act self-righteously. I tried hard to be good enough for God to love and accept me, and was frustrated with my failures to do so.

Richard Lovelace has pointed out that too many Christians base their justification (their standing before God) on their sanctification (their growth in becoming more like Christ)[1]. I'll bet that's true of you, at least some

---

1. Richard Lovelace, *Dynamics of Spiritual Life*, (Downers Grove, IVP,

of the time. Compare a day where you're especially obedient with a day where you're especially sinful.[2] Maybe on the first day you are very close to God, but on the second you are caught up in pornography and masturbation. On which of those days do you feel like you can approach God? Do you feel like you can just stroll into His presence on that second day? Probably not; in your heart, you think that God sees you differently on the first day than He does on the second. The Bible teaches us that this is not true at all!

You are no more worthy of God's love and acceptance on the first day than you are on the second. And you are no more worthy of His judgment on the second day than you are on the first.

Why do we have such a hard time believing both of those statements? You might be surprised to find out that the same part of your nature that decided to get into porn also wants to take responsibility for your change in getting away from it. The same sinful nature that lusts after women also wants to reform you.

In Galatians 3:3, Paul asks, "Are you so foolish? Having begun by the Spirit, are you now being perfected by the flesh?" This verse gets to the heart of our issue. We've begun our relationship with God by the Spirit but we want to obey Him by our own self-effort. We would

---

1979) p. 211 – "We all automatically gravitate toward the assumption that we are justified by our level of sanctification, and when this posture is adopted it inevitably focuses our attention not on Christ but on the adequacy of our own obedience."

2. I am indebted to Jerry Bridges for this illustration; see his book *The Disciplines of Grace* (Colorado Springs: NavPress, 2006) for a somewhat different treatment of this idea

like to think that we want to obey God because we love Him and want to follow Him, but underneath it all, we really want to be the ones who take the credit for our improvement. This is what it means to be "perfected by the flesh."

If I change by my own power, I ultimately get the credit. I want to look good before others: "Look at me! Look how well I'm doing!" Do you see it? It's nothing more than sinful pride masquerading as spirituality. What a trap!

Let's see this at work on that second day. After you've spent time looking at porn, you feel ashamed and hopeless. It's at this phase that the Law plays its role: you've sinned, you've violated your conscience, you've told yourself you wouldn't do it again, but you did, and now on top of the realization that you've done wrong, your religious heart jumps up and begins telling you what a sinner you are! What does that look like?

- I can't believe I did that again! (see Jeremiah 17:9 for a refutation)
- Next time I'll stop before it goes that far! (see James 1:15)
- God can't love/use me when I still do this! (see Romans 9:16)

Our sin shames us, and simultaneously our sinful hearts accuse us, wanting to take control of the situation, to exclude God from being our sole provider. We fell into sin because we trusted ourselves, and we foolishly trust ourselves to get out. We think that if we only try harder, or care about our wives more, or serve the Lord enough, our sin problem will just go away. In fact, trusting yourself for these things will just send you deeper into addiction. Our problem is not that we aren't trying hard enough; our problem is that we want to trust ourselves instead of God for the power to change. We may believe that we are trusting God but we lie to ourselves and continue on in our determined self-effort and pride. As a result, we live as hypocrites in a state of deceit.

The practice of deceit

"Behold, the wicked man conceives evil and is pregnant with mischief and gives birth to lies. He makes a pit, digging it out, and falls into the hole that he has made." (Psalm 7:14-15)

When we believe that we have the power in ourselves to overcome sin, we actively believe a lie by placing ourselves (rather than God) at the center of our need to change. We either make vows and promises to try harder, or we make rationalizations; we try to obey God, but when we can't, we cover it up. Let me give you a couple of examples of the lies that we tell ourselves.

- "That will be the last time I do this."
- "I'll do better tomorrow."
- "I'm not really hurting anybody."
- "At least it's been a long time since my last time."
- "I've had a really bad day – I deserve this."

The demands of God's perfect law are so great that if we try to live by them we will either be completely miserable, or we'll put on a show. Lying to people is the inevitable result of a life lived under law.

When I came out with my confession of my addiction to pornography, my friend Chris recommended that I read the book *Till We Have Faces*, by C.S. Lewis. I read this book on the plane as I traveled on a business trip, and I kept wondering what it had to do with my problem with pornography. The story is a retelling of the Greek myth of Cupid and Psyche, and one of its primary ideas is that a person must be real and honest with themselves and others before they can receive divine revelation, As Lewis puts it, "How can the gods meet us face to face till we have faces?"

When I asked my friend why he recommended this cryptic book he laid it on me: "Brian, your problem is that you're a liar." Those words stung me like a slap in the face. Everything within me rose up to defend myself. A liar? How could he say that? I couldn't think of a worse reputation to have, and my self-righteous heart was enraged and hurt. I protested, "Lying is not my problem; lust is." Chris quietly persisted: "Your real problem is lying: you have been lying to me, your wife, and your friends."

He was right of course. I had a *persona*: a false self that I presented for the public that I thought would be acceptable to others. The persona is smart, witty, self-confident, rational, and wise. The persona might have looked at pornography in the past, but he's doing pretty well with that whole thing now. The persona loves and honors his wife. But what's the real person like? The real person is sneaky, fearful, rebellious, subjective and foolish. The real person has done some really shameful things. The real person is not someone to be admired and looked up to. I had to be broken of my trust in myself and see myself as the sinner that I am. I had to acknowledge my desperate need of mercy before I could be changed.

The problem of internal solutions

Legalism, or performance-based solutions to sin problems, allows us to believe that we are not that bad. We are still good enough to save ourselves. God wants us to see that we are completely without hope apart from Christ. Only by the grace of Christ can we stand at all for one single second.

> "The Lord saw how great man's wickedness on the earth had become, and that every inclination of the thoughts of his heart was only evil all the time." (Genesis 6:5) "The fool says in his heart, "There is no God." They are corrupt, their deeds are vile; there is no one who does good. The Lord looks down from heaven on the sons of men to see if there are any who understand, any who seek God. All have turned aside, they have together become corrupt; there is no one who does good, not even one." (Psalm 14:1-3)

The Bible's teaching about the sinful nature of man is not meant to make us hopeless. Instead, it is intended to liberate us from thinking that we can do anything to save ourselves, or thinking that we can please God by our own efforts. Until we understand that we can contribute nothing to our own holiness, we will continue

to experience failure and defeat. You have to give up on
yourself in order to be changed by grace!

For the person who is struggling with pornography,
this type of failure could drive you back into your addiction; it's tempting to numb the pain of defeat with more
porn. It is for this reason that so many Christians are
defeated: their efforts to control or manage this problem
have only made it worse. Even if you manage to keep it
together, your pride will sink you.

In his 1741 sermon, The Method of Grace, George
Whitefield said:

> "Before you can [know you are at peace with God],
> you must not only be troubled for your sins of your
> life, but also for the sins of your best duties and
> performances... Before you can be at peace with
> God, there must be a deep conviction before you
> can be brought out of your self-righteousness; it
> is the last idol taken out of our heart. The pride of
> our heart will not let us submit to the righteousness
> of Jesus Christ. But if you never felt that you had
> no righteousness of your own, if you never felt the
> deficiency of your own righteousness you cannot
> come to Jesus Christ."

The Turning Point

So what are we supposed to do? We need changed
thinking. Rather than thinking that we have an external
problem (outside temptations, my background) with an
internal solution (my own self-efforts to change), we need
to see that we have an internal problem (we are sinners),
for which the only solution is outside of ourselves.

In fact, once we have arrived at the point where we see our sin, our idolatry, the hollowness of our lies, and the utter impossibility of ever living up to God's holy standard, we can't just give up!

We have to move toward the forgiveness and grace and mercy of God. That solution is only found in Jesus Christ and his cross. Maybe you don't have what it takes, but Jesus does, and he offers his righteousness freely to those who receive Him.

If you've received Christ as savior, you must put aside any thought of God's judgment. If his acceptance was based on anything that we could do, we are all lost, from the best to the worst of us. The severity of your sin is not the issue, because the death of Christ is sufficient for all of our sins.

We're going to spend considerable time throughout the course of this book discussing the platform of grace upon which we must stand in order to have victory. God has given us everything that we need to live lives of meaning and purpose. While we will never live perfect sinless lives on this side of heaven, we can have substantial victory over besetting sins, like pornography, fantasy, and masturbation. Better yet, we can live victoriously for him, giving glory to Christ.

> "His divine power has given us everything we need for life and godliness through our knowledge of him who called us by his own glory and goodness. Through these he has given us his very great and precious promises, so that through them you may participate in the divine nature and escape

the corruption in the world caused by evil desires."
(2 Peter 1:3-4)

God has given us his promises so that through them we can participate in His nature. These promises — that Christ died for our sins once for all time, that we will be with Him forever, that His Spirit will be in us, empowering us to live holy lives in the midst of darkness — have the power to change us. This change does not come from knowing the promises, or claiming the promises, but rather from our acts of faith, living our lives as if these things were true of us because they are true of us.

Things in our favor

Of greatest significance, we have the gospel of the grace of God, who accepts us totally. We are accepted not because of what we have done, but because of the death of Jesus Christ, his son. If you have received that gift, God has forgiven you, regardless of what you have done, are doing right now, and are going to do. God's forgiveness is a settled fact, and nothing you can do will change his disposition toward you. "He who did not spare his own Son but gave him up for us all, how will he not also with him graciously give us all things?" (Romans 8:32)

You need to come to grips with who you are before God. It's your standing before God that matters the most. If he loves and accepts you, then he can give you the power to overcome sin. This is the primary power of change: you must act, but with his power, not your own.

Perhaps you picked up this book because of your struggles with pornography, but all this talk of Jesus and the cross is not something you understand or accept. Let's pause to consider some basic ideas about the gospel of Jesus Christ.

God created us perfect, without all the problems we see in the world today, but we decided to rebel against him, and that decision changed us. Our rebellion cut us off from his life, which was intended to sustain us and kept us whole. We began to follow our own course, a course based on selfishness. Since we were never designed to be totally self-directed we found bondage instead of freedom. We began looking for what we had lost in things that could never be God, things like power and lust and possessions.

Because God is altogether holy and perfect, he could not just sit back without doing something about our rebellion against him and our violation of one another. It was his standard that we disobeyed. That disobedience was personal, not just judicial. The sentence handed down upon the whole human race was death: physical death, and spiritual death.

However, God is also the most loving being imaginable. Therefore, he made it possible for you to come back into relationship with him. He sent his son, Jesus Christ, to live the perfect life that we didn't live, and to pay the penalty for our rebellion. He exchanged his righteousness for our sin, so that we could have his righteousness and live.

The result of this exchange is that we are set free from bondage to selfishness, and are given a new life. To have this life, you simply have to receive it: it's a gift – that's what we call grace. The grace of God is the foundation of all real change. If you have never asked him for that gift, do it now! You don't have to change your life to receive this gift; it is the very gift itself that will change you.

In addition to God's grace, we have the power of the truth, which is the Word of God. God's truth transforms our thinking, which in turn can transform our lives as we exercise our faith, living in obedience to the truth that can make you free. As we saw above in the verse from 2 Peter, as we live our lives trusting in "his precious and very great promises" we "become partakers of the divine nature." This is no magical formula where we learn a few Bible verses and are instantly transformed; you have to devote yourself to being absorbed in the Word and putting it into practice as the Spirit of God teaches you.

We have the community of the saints. God has given us brothers and sisters with whom we can share our sorrows, temptations, and joys. I hope that you are studying this book in a group setting, where you can experience the grace of God through the acceptance and counsel of others. It is essential for the growth of any Christian to be a part of real community, and to be an active participant, not just a spectator in the corporate life of the Church. Building fulfilling relationships is important, but you also have a critical role to play.

We also have the indwelling power of the Holy Spirit.

"You, however, are not in the flesh but in the Spirit, if in fact the Spirit of God dwells in you...[and] if Christ is in you, although the body is dead because of sin, the Spirit is life because of righteousness. If the Spirit of him who raised Jesus from the dead dwells in you, he who raised Christ Jesus from the dead will also give life to your mortal bodies through his Spirit who dwells in you." (Romans 8:9-11)

All the power that is needed for you to live according to God's design is yours through the Spirit, whom the Father gives to all who receive him. Instead of being corrupted by lust, the Spirit makes it possible for us to be more like God. The amazing thing is that we already have all of this, it's not something we have to ask for: God has done it for us at the cross!

These gifts from God are the basis for our growth in Christ, and provide the means for our release from the power of sin, no matter how deeply ingrained. Your own legalistic self-effort will never yield anything like the power of God working through his truth in the context of real, loving community. We will study each of these in more detail, but right now you need to see that the hope that is available through Christ applies to you.

He will never leave you or forsake you, and he is committed to lovingly see you through this issue in your life. Let God convince you that this is true, and rejoice in him for the gift of his Son!

For Group Discussion

Since you last met together, has there been progress in your life, or have you struggled with failure? Let each person share his story.

In what ways have you tried, but failed, to move toward victory in your fight against sexual sin and pornography? What might be some reasons that your previous attempts have failed?

In what ways have you lied to yourself in this area of sexual sin? In what ways have you lied to others? What do you think motivates us to lie to ourselves and others? What is the real truth that counteracts the lies that you have held in your heart? Are there any Scriptures that you know that would back that up?

Pray for each member in your group. Pray that God would uncover where you relate to him legalistically, and rejoice in him that now you are sons, not slaves.

FOUR

COSTLY GRACE

"*I was steeped in pornography all through my middle school and high school years. It wasn't until I really understood what grace was that I began to get victory in this area.*

I still remember vividly the last night I viewed pornography: I was sitting in my chair and tangibly sensed a distance between me and God that I had never experienced before. I had grown very close to God over the past year. I was starting to realize the effect that my sin had on my relationship with God. Not only was it negatively affecting the way I viewed women, it was distancing me from the man who gave His life as a ransom for me. It brought me to tears knowing that God had not distanced Himself from me. He had already done everything necessary to bring me into a relationship with Him. I was choosing to reject His love, and that caused the marked sense of distance between us.

When I truly began to understand what it meant that God had nailed every sin of mine on the cross, I experienced an overwhelming sense of freedom. I had the ability for the first time in my life to come before God and my friends and admit that I was unable to pull myself out of the hole I had dug, and that I needed Christ's death on the cross to empower me."

U p to this point we've seen the problem of pornography in our lives and culture. We've looked at the ways porn damages your thinking as well as your relationship with God and others. We've also seen how any attempt to address the problem in your own strength inevitably leads to failure and a sense of deepening shame that will eventually drive most of us further into addiction.

We need a way to deal with this problem that goes beyond managing day-to-day behaviors. You need change at the very root of your being, a change of heart that will affect the orientation of your whole life. That change comes through the astonishing grace of God.

Real change in the life of the believer comes from the power of the gospel of grace, and is based on the finished work of Christ on the cross. In this chapter, we're going to explore amazing grace — how the grace of God changes everything. It can liberate you from enslavement to addicting sin and set you free to experience a life of genuine fulfillment.

What is grace?

The word *grace* in the Bible refers to a free gift, something that is unmerited. When we say, "salvation is a free gift" we mean that salvation comes to us as a gift from God; it can't be earned and is not deserved; what we deserve is judgment for our rebellion against God. We receive the grace of God with the empty hands of faith. God does all of the work of salvation for us.

> "For while we were still weak, at the right time
> Christ died for the ungodly. For one will scarcely
> die for a righteous person—though perhaps for

a good person one would dare even to die— but God shows his love for us in that while we were still sinners, Christ died for us. Since, therefore, we have now been justified by his blood, much more shall we be saved by him from the wrath of God. For if while we were enemies we were reconciled to God by the death of his Son, much more, now that we are reconciled, shall we be saved by his life." (Romans 5:6–10)

Paul is describing the condition of each one of us outside of grace: we were weak, we were sinners, and we were enemies. We were too weak to save ourselves. We are sinners, and as such cannot approach God. God declared as much to Moses when he said, "No one can see me and live" (Exodus 33:20). At the same time we were enemies – we didn't really want to approach God anyway. Paul had already described this earlier in the book of Romans, "None is righteous, no, not one; no one understands; no one seeks for God" (Romans 3:10–11).

The magnitude of the gift is measured by considering our total lack of merit to receive it. All that you and I deserve is hell—a life now and forever apart from God—because on our own, we cannot conform to God's holiness or morality, and on our own, we really cherish our sin life. Nonetheless, it is in this state of conscious and subconscious rebellion that grace comes to us. By freely offering salvation to sinners, God has taken the initiative in grace where we could not and would not. Grace is God seeking us, his enemies, with love.

Charles Spurgeon put it this way: "the offended God himself in infinite compassion broke the silence, and came forth to bless his enemies."[1]

Grace is the context for all believers with regards to their standing before God. It is how he sees you and how he deals with you at every moment of your life. A holy and just God cannot see sinners as sons except by grace. The grievous harm we have done to others looms between God and you. Not only is there much evil that you have done, there is much good that you have not done. Only by grace can God relate in love toward you. Once you receive grace it becomes the only foundation you stand on before him. The barrier that your sin once presented is removed.

Grace comes to us from God the Father, but can only be found "in Christ."

> [God...] saved us and called us to a holy calling, not because of our works but because of his own purpose and grace, which he gave us in Christ Jesus before the ages began. (2 Timothy 1:9)

> I give thanks to my God always for you because of the grace of God that was given you in Christ Jesus. (1 Corinthians 1:4)

> For the law was given through Moses; grace and truth came through Jesus Christ. (John 1:17)

Jesus is the embodiment of the grace of God primarily because of what he did on the cross. If you've ever

1. Charles Spurgeon, "The Great Birthday and our Coming of Age" (sermon No. 1815)

wondered, "Does God love me?" you need only look upon the one who took your sins upon himself, suffered God's wrath for them in your place, and offered you eternal life in return. In grace he loved you by giving you himself.

> "Grace is not a 'thing'. It is not a substance that can be measured or a commodity to be distributed. It is the 'grace of the Lord Jesus Christ' (2 Corinthians 13:14). In essence, it is Jesus Himself."[2]

Grace describes all of the ways that God deals with us: in calling us to himself, in paying the penalty for our sin, in uniting us with Christ in his death and resurrection, in releasing us from bondage to sin and Satan, in leading and guiding us through life, in teaching us to love others, in every patient dealing with us. In all these ways it is always by grace, always a gift from the love of God. Grace is God's love in action toward us.

Grace is what will make the biggest difference as you seek freedom from sexual sin. When you stop making excuses, stop lying to yourself and others, stop trying to reform yourself, and open yourself up to see the magnitude of your sin, God can reveal the depths of the moral sewer that runs in your divided heart. Grace then calls to you, "Come all of you who are weary and heavy-laden, and I will give you rest" (Matthew 11:28). We find rest from sin at the oddest of places—a place of gruesome torment and death—the cross of Jesus Christ. Here we find forgiveness for our sins. As Jesus takes our judgment and death on himself, we receive his life as a gift.

---

2. Sinclair Ferguson, *By Grace Alone* (Lake Mary, FL: Reformation Trust Publishing, 2010), xv

The means of the grace we have received is the cross of Christ, and it is here that we best see divine love in action. The cross didn't "happen" to Jesus as a result of the offense of his radical message; God planned it from the beginning, and the Father orchestrated the sequence of events surrounding the execution of Jesus. The early church understood that the cross was in the plan of God, and that his plan had been set forth from before time. God decided before anything was created that he would send his Son to redeem mankind. (See Acts 4:27-28; 2 Timothy 1:9)

The love of God planned the only way out of man's dilemma. He would undo the damage that we had done to ourselves and our world, and in so doing make it possible for the relationship between us and God to be restored.

How do we get it?

What happens to us at the cross? In its simplest terms, the cross creates the possibility for forgiveness for our sins, peace with God, release from the ruling power of sin, and a new life. As we study the New Testament, we find that the doctrines of the cross are multi-faceted. No one picture can sum up all that God has done to bring us salvation, and this short chapter will not do justice to the topic. Instead, we'll look at a brief overview of those things which are so essential to understanding what God has done through Jesus.[3]

The doctrines of justification and identification with

---

3. For further reading, I would recommend *The Gospel for Real Life*, by Jerry Bridges, *The Cross of Christ*, by John Stott, and *Death By Love*, by Mark Driscoll.

Christ are of great importance in explaining how grace releases us from the penalty and power of sin. These doctrines are not just of interest to theologians; they affect you as you seek freedom from sin. These principles form the lifeblood of your day-to-day walk with God in grace.

Our Justification

> For all have sinned and fall short of the glory of God, and are justified by his grace as a gift, through the redemption that is in Christ Jesus, whom God put forward as a propitiation by his blood, to be received by faith. (Romans 3:23–25)

Our justification means that we are no longer guilty before God; we have been declared righteous, as righteous as Christ himself. Our sins have been paid for, and God declares us both "not guilty" and "righteous." The charges were not dropped; instead, the penalty for sin has been fully paid, and we can never be condemned again (Romans 8:1). This was accomplished through redemption by propitiation.

Redemption is a word that means to be set free, or ransomed. In Roman society you would pay a ransom to release someone who had been kidnapped, or to emancipate a slave. This word also had meaning for the Jewish audience of the time, as it was the word used to describe how God had set Israel free from their bondage in Egypt (Exodus 6:6). In the New Testament, redemption refers to our being set free from slavery to sin (Titus 2:14) by the forgiveness of our sins (Ephesians 1:7). We have been bought out of slavery and set free "by his blood."

Redemption is also used in reference to our being set free from the demands of the law. "Christ redeemed us from the curse of the law by becoming a curse for us—for it is written, "Cursed is everyone who is hanged on a tree" (Galatians 3:13). The law, the expression of the holy character of God, demanded a price for sin, and that price was paid in full for each one of us. After suffering the staggering wrath of God for all of human sin, Jesus cried out, "it is finished!" — the debt was fully paid.

Our redemption was accomplished through "propitiation by his blood." Propitiation is a word that meant "satisfaction of wrath" in the Roman culture of Paul's day. It was often used to refer to the wrath of the Roman gods. In Jewish culture it was the Greek word used to describe the mercy seat (hilasterion) used in the Day of Atonement.

Some people have a problem with the idea of the wrath of God; we don't like to think of God as an angry God. God's anger isn't like our anger; his wrath is based on his perfect goodness and sense of justice. Through the sacrifice of Christ on the cross, the wrath of God has been fully exhausted. The terrible "cup" of God's wrath against you has been poured out on his Son (John 18:11; Mark 14:36; John 19:30). Jesus willingly drank the cup that was meant for you. Propitiation means that God is not mad any more about your sin. His justice has been satisfied, and his anger toward your sin has been exhausted.

Full payment for the wrath of God has been made on your behalf "by his blood." Just as the blood of the bull and the goat sacrificed on the Day of Atonement covered the mercy seat for the sins of the people in ancient Israel, (Leviticus 16:14–15) so too the blood of Jesus covers our sins, and God is satisfied with the payment that was made. For God to have any wrath towards those He has forgiven would be a violation of His character, because the debt has been paid, once for all. If you are a Christian, any fear that you might have of God's wrath towards you is unfounded.

Propitiation matters, because we can be confident to enter the presence of God, regardless of our sins, whether we have sinned with pornography, or anger, or pride. All has been paid for in Christ, and as a result, we are "justified" before God – he sees us as though we were as righteous as Jesus, and any hostility between he and us has been removed.

> Therefore, since we have been justified by faith, we have peace with God through our Lord Jesus Christ. Through him we have also obtained access by faith into this grace in which we stand, and we rejoice in hope of the glory of God. (Romans 5:1-2)

As a result of our justification, we have peace with God. Our standing before God is based on his work of grace, not our works or good deeds. We can rejoice in the certainty of our final acceptance by God at the end of our lives where we will be transformed into the likeness of his glory.

This, then, is the basis for your walk with God, no matter what sins you are struggling with. Unless you can see that this applies to you, you will always either try to stand before God based on your own good works, or shrink back from him in fear. Either one of those will lead you to failure.

"Only a fraction of the present body of professing
Christians are solidly appropriating the justifying
work of Christ in their lives... In their day-to-day
existence they rely on their sanctification for justification... Few know enough to start each day with
a thoroughgoing stand upon Luther's platform: you
are accepted, looking outward in faith and claiming
the wholly alien righteousness of Christ as the only
ground for acceptance, relaxing in that quality of
trust which will produce increasing sanctification
as faith is active in love and gratitude."[4]

What a difference this is from the sad state of many
Christians! They are plagued by sin and defeated rather
than experiencing the victory of what Christ has done
for them at the cross. They live lives of "quiet desperation and go to the grave with the song still in them" as
Thoreau said. Porn can do that to you. Rather than joining your voice with Jesus in the song of his glory, you
sing feebly and alone to the false god Eros. It is a sad
anthem that leaves your heart empty while the one you
were meant to sing is slowly forgotten.

You were meant for better things than that! You were
meant to experience the fullness of the peace of God that
justification brings. No matter what you did yesterday,
you can get up each morning in hopeful gratitude for
what Christ has done for you.

---

4. Richard Lovelace, *Dynamics of Spiritual Life* (Downers Grove, IVP,
1979), 101-102

Identification with Christ

These doctrines relating to the cross of Christ have a remarkable result: we have been identified, or united with Christ. Your union with Christ is one of the most important things to understand, especially as you face the onslaught of sin and temptation.

Our identity, and our understanding of it, will affect our behavior. We see this acted out in other areas of life. If your identity is "surfer" the things you value, what you wear, say, and do will be quite different than if your identity is "accountant." We all act out of what we believe ourselves to be. If you are a Christian, the Bible tells you that you have a different identity than before.

> I have been crucified with Christ. It is no longer I who live, but Christ who lives in me. And the life I now live in the flesh I live by faith in the Son of God, who loved me and gave himself for me. (Galatians 2:20)

> What shall we say then? Are we to continue in sin that grace may abound? By no means! How can we who died to sin still live in it? Do you not know that all of us who have been baptized into Christ Jesus were baptized into his death? We were buried therefore with him by baptism into death, in order that, just as Christ was raised from the dead by the glory of the Father, we too might walk in newness of life. (Romans 6:1–4)

The fact that we "died with Christ" has made a fundamental change in our identity, one that makes continuing under the dominion of sin inconsistent with who we really are. How can we who died to sin still live in it? That's the question that flows from a new identity.

In the movie Trading Places Eddie Murphy plays a homeless street hustler who is made managing director of a corporation. Though he dresses the part of a rich man, and tries to act out his new role, he is still the same person underneath the expensive suits. A lot of Christians see our new identity this way: you are a Christian now, so you should act the part. There is a big difference here, however. Our new status renders us fundamentally changed; we've been released from the power, or dominion of sin.

> "We know that our old self was crucified with him
> in order that the body of sin might be brought to
> nothing, so that we would no longer be enslaved
> to sin." (Romans 6:6)

The Greek word for "brought to nothing," or as some translations put it, "done away with" is *katargeo*, which in this context means deprived of power. Prior to being a Christian, sin reigned over you, held you in bondage, and had full dominion over your life. That power has now been broken, and sin can no longer rule you.

So many of us feel helpless against the temptations of sin, yet the reigning control of sin is no longer essential to our nature. Sin can be *invested* with power over us, but it is not *intrinsic* to us any more. Paul tells us that it is our choice to either let sin reign, or to live by faith in the righteousness that Christ has given us.

> "Let not sin therefore reign in your mortal body, to
> make you obey its passions. Do not present your
> members to sin as instruments for unrighteousness,

but present yourselves to God as those who have been brought from death to life, and your members to God as instruments for righteousness. For sin will have no dominion over you, since you are not under law but under grace." (Romans 6:12–14)

Because we are truly free in a way that we were never before, we have a choice of what or whom to serve. Our freedom is not the modern American view of freedom, where we think we are fully self-directed, and we can do whatever we please. "The man who imagines he is free, because he acknowledges no god but his own ego, is deluded; for the service of one's own ego is the very essence of slavery to sin."[5] We are by nature subservient beings, either serving God or sin.

"Sinning does not prove one's freedom, much less make one free. Ironically, sin, once committed, does not aid one to become one's own master, but rather proceeds to become one's master; sin reigns as lord in the fallen creature."[6]

Before becoming a Christian, obeying the passions of the sinful nature was the only choice you had; according to the Bible you were a slave to sin. Now that sin's ruling power has been broken, you have a choice to continue to subject yourself to sin's dominion and thus deny your new nature, or to present yourself to God as his adopted son, and commit your life to living for him.

---

5. C.E.B. Cranfield, *A Critical and Exegetical Commentary on the Epistle to the Romans*, (London, T&T Clark Ltd., 1975), 323
6. Ben Witherington, *Paul's Letter to the Romans*, (Grand Rapids, Eerdmans, 2004), 165

Sin is still present in you and will take the opportunity to rule if you let it. If you're caught in the grip of lust, you have given sin dominion in your life. Therefore you are obeying its passions and you're presenting the members of your body to sin as instruments of sin. Here is where you have a choice: instead of allowing sin to reign you can stand on the fact of your new identity and present yourself to God as one who is alive from the dead.

Resurrection and Regeneration

> "You, however, are not in the flesh but in the Spirit, if in fact the Spirit of God dwells in you. Anyone who does not have the Spirit of Christ does not belong to him. But if Christ is in you, although the body is dead because of sin, the Spirit is life because of righteousness. If the Spirit of him who raised Jesus from the dead dwells in you, he who raised Christ Jesus from the dead will also give life to your mortal bodies through his Spirit who dwells in you." (Romans 8:9–11)

Because Christ rose from the dead to new life, you too can be raised to a new life, given a new nature (2 Corinthians 5:17), and invested with the life of the Spirit of God. This new life is the fulfillment of the promise Jesus made to his disciples.

> And I will ask the Father, and he will give you another Helper, to be with you forever, even the Spirit of truth, whom the world cannot receive, because it neither sees him nor knows him. You know him, for he dwells with you and will be in

you. I will not leave you as orphans; I will come
to you. (John 14:16–18)

The Spirit of God, the third Person of the Trinity, has
come to you and taken up residence in your heart. He is
the active agent of grace in your daily life. It is he who:

- regenerates and renews us (Titus 3:5)
- indwells us (Romans 8:9)
- places us into Christ and the church
  (Galatians 3:27; 1 Corinthians 12:13)
- seals us in Christ (Ephesians 1:13-14)
- assures us of our salvation (Romans 8:15-16)
- shows us the meaning of God's word
  (1 Corinthians 2:12)
- leads us into holy living (Galatians 5:16-17)
- empowers us (Romans 8:11)
- gives us hope about the future (Romans 15:13)
- prays for us (Romans 8:26-27)

The Holy Spirit is the agent of change in our lives.
His presence in us has a tremendous impact on our inclinations, our desires — the things that matter to us. Before
we met Christ, we were unable to care about God or His
agenda for our lives. Now that we have God's Spirit living
inside of us, we can understand God's will as expressed
in the Bible, and we can begin to take its direction as
our own. Our desires, which were previously oriented
towards self, can be transformed into a new desire for
holiness, and love for God and others.

How Do We Walk in Grace?

As Christians we "have" this grace. However, it is possible for our present experience of grace to be deficient. You may have been taught that you gain your approval from God on the basis of your performance. Perhaps you see grace as a free pass to do whatever you want. Maybe you are somewhere in between. Wherever you're at right now, you have a continual need to "grow in the grace and knowledge of our Lord and Savior Jesus Christ." (2 Peter 3:18)

The gospel isn't just something that we accept in order to become Christians, and then forget about afterwards. Paul says that the gospel is "of first importance" (1 Corinthians 15:3). The gospel is the key to the Christian life, for the rest of your life. As you seek freedom from sexual bondage, the cross of Christ will be the place you find it every day. If you want to experience the power of grace, you will need to become deeply acquainted with the Bible's teaching on it.

> ". . .the gospel, which has come to you, as indeed
> in the whole world it is bearing fruit and grow-
> ing—as it also does among you, since the day you
> heard it and understood the grace of God in truth"
> (Colossians 1:5–7)

The gospel bears fruit and grows in our lives and within our churches. It is the basis for our spiritual growth. Those "precious and magnificent promises" by which we become partakers of the divine nature mostly concern what Christ has done for us. In order to appropriate those transforming promises you need to become absorbed in them. For the person who struggles with sexual temptation and experiences failure, gaining a growing confidence in the forgiveness of our sins is key. As long as we are held captive by guilt and shame, we will never find rest and freedom. Martin Luther said,

> "The troubled conscience, in view of God's judgment, has no remedy against desperation and eternal death, unless it takes hold of the forgiveness of sins by grace, freely offered in Christ Jesus, which if it can apprehend, it may then be at rest... I rest only upon that righteousness, which is the righteousness of Christ and of the Holy Ghost."[7]

We must hold on tight to our position and identity in grace and not let go. Accepting and believing these facts will be a daily battle for many of you, and this is where the regular study of God's word is so important. We will talk more fully about the role of God's word in chapter 6.

William Newell, in his Romans commentary, has a section called A Few Words About Grace. In it he talks about the proper attitudes we should have under grace. Here are just a few points that apply to our standing with God:

- To believe, and to consent to be loved while unworthy, is the great secret.
- To expect to be blessed, though realizing more and more lack of worth.
- To be disappointed with yourself is to have believed in yourself.

7. Martin Luther, *Commentary on Galatians*, (Grand Rapids, Fleming Revell, 1988), 19

- To be discouraged is unbelief — as to God's purpose and plan of blessing for you.
- The lack of Divine blessing, therefore, comes from unbelief, and not from failure of devotion.
- Real devotion to God arises, not from man's will to show it; but from the discovery that blessing has been received from God while we were yet unworthy and undevoted.

It is also important to "set our minds on the Spirit" and not on the flesh. This has to do with our focus. Those of us who have struggled with sexual sin can easily focus our attention solely on this problem and make it the point of our Christian lives to prevent this sin. This inevitably leads to a defeated attitude and depression, because we can never eradicate sin totally, even though we must wage war against it determinedly.

You need to focus on the blessings of the gospel more than you do the calamity of sin. Paul tells Timothy to "be strengthened by the grace that is in Christ Jesus." (2 Timothy 2:1) and the writer of Hebrews tells us that "it is good for the heart to be strengthened by grace" (Hebrews 13:9) Much of this has to do with what you focus on, what you become passionate about, what fills your mind. Emphasis is important.

- Focus on salvation instead of sin
- Focus on grace instead of guilt
- Focus on your freedom instead of your fallenness
- Focus on love instead of law

The whole point of turning from sin is to turn towards God, experiencing his blessings, delighting in him as your true satisfaction, and living a full life of loving service to him.

"Turn my eyes from looking at worthless things; and give me life in your ways." (Psalm 119:37)

For Group Discussion

Talk about how things have been going since you last met. Try to share humbly and honestly — are you seeing small victories, a renewed conscience? Is there still sin that you have not confessed? If you've had victory, rejoice in it!

How does the free gift of your justification affect you? Knowing that your Father in heaven will not condemn you, do you feel more or less inclined toward sexual sin?

How could you use Scripture in this chapter, or others that you know about the grace of God, in your struggle with sexual sin?

What kind of steps would "presenting yourself to God" and your whole person as "instruments of righteousness" look like for you?

Pray for each member in your group, asking for strength and courage for those who are struggling, and thanking God for those are who seeing progress. Pray for "enlightened hearts" to see God's manifold grace.

FIVE

ALL OF LIFE IS REPENTANCE

One of the students in the college ministry at Xenos Christian Fellowship told me,

> *"I began to notice that after getting into pornography, there was an overbearing, overwhelming sense of guilt. The worse and guiltier I felt about my sin, the more it had a grip on me, and I realized that this guilt and shame was precisely, "the sorrow of the world." (2 Cor. 7:10) I knew that I had to break free from this endless cycle if I wanted to have victory in this area. For me, true repentance began when I sat before God and agreed with everything that He said was true about me, and my addiction. When I was tempted in ways that to this day still feel unbearable, I responded to my temptation with truth from God's word that I had digested many times over. Eventually, these truths became real in my experience, and I have been free for almost three years now."*

"Our Lord and Master Jesus Christ…willed that the whole life of believers should be repentance" Martin Luther, the first of the 95 Theses

When I was a non-Christian I lived my life totally for myself, totally in rebellion against God who still pursued me with his grace. My life was characterized by the sins that were typical at a southern California college:

the drugs, drinking parties, and sex. I had grown up in a rather strict home in the Bay Area, and being away at school in Los Angeles was like being dropped into a sensual Disneyland where there was no admission fee, and the park never closed. My whole life seemed oriented around pleasure.

I became a Christian while living in a fraternity house at UCLA in my sophomore year. As a new believer I understood what repentance was: I had lived a life of sensuality and now wanted to live for Jesus. I stopped using drugs and sleeping around; I started studying the Bible and sharing my newfound faith. At that time, repentance meant that I had changed the orientation of my life. It was a turning from sin and a turning towards Jesus. I'm sure that some of your stories are like mine.

What I didn't realize until much later was that repentance was not just something I needed as I went from being a non-Christian to becoming a Christian. Repentance was supposed to continue, and become deeper and more comprehensive. Like Luther said, repentance should characterize my whole life.

Repentance is a vital part of our active participation in the grace of God because it puts God in His place and keeps us in ours. As we grow in Christ we will develop an ever-increasing awareness of the holiness of God as well as a growing awareness of the presence of indwelling sin in our own hearts. Over time, this difference becomes more and more apparent. *Repentance is the heartfelt acknowledgement of this difference.*

For those of us who have sinned sexually, the practice of repentance is critical. You can't be involved in such damaging sin and just shrug it off with, "oh well, I'm forgiven, so it's OK." Those of you with more sensitive consciences may not be saying that. Perhaps instead you substitute guilt and penance for true repentance. Feeling guilty or trying to pay God back will never bring the change of heart attitude that he desires. "Behold, you delight in truth in the inward being, and you teach me wisdom in the secret heart." (Psalm 51:6)Additionally, I fear that many of us default to a cavalier attitude towards our sin. Having accepted the grace of Christ, we could assume that how we live doesn't matter, or that since there are always worse sinners than us, our sins are insignificant by comparison. We fail to see how deep sin runs within us, how it affects others, and how it affects our relationship with God.

In his book, *Revival*, D. Martyn Lloyd-Jones said:

> "Be careful how you treat God, my friends. You may say to yourself, 'I can sin against God and then, of course, I can repent and go back and find God whenever I want him.' You try it. And you will sometimes find that not only can you not find God, but that you do not even want to. You will be aware of a terrible hardness in your heart. And you can do nothing about it. And then you suddenly realize that it is God punishing you in order to reveal your sinfulness and your vileness to you. And there is only one thing to do. You turn back to him and you say, 'O God, do not go on dealing with me judicially, though I deserve it. Soften my heart. Melt me. I cannot do it myself.' You

cast yourself utterly upon his mercy and upon his compassion."[1]

Repentance starts with God's conviction in our hearts. The Holy Spirit shows us our sin and deepens our understanding of it, not to make us feel guilty, but rather to draw us nearer to God. This too has to be a work of grace: we are easily blinded by our sin and have a hard time seeing how it affects our lives and our relationship with God and others. Because conviction of sin is by grace, you don't have to go looking for it: God will reveal it to you.

> "Is there any point of controversy between you and God? I refer of course to real, known issues. If there is nothing special, then there is no need for you to search around to find something; the Lord himself will always discover it. When he wants to bring to light something you are overlooking, he will always point his finger there, and you will know it. There is no need for you to turn your eyes within and by checking up and analyzing every feeling to try to dig it out. Just praise him! It is the Lord's business, not yours, to shine into your heart and show you when you are astray from him."[2]

I have heard some Bible teachers say that repentance means simply to "change your mind", an interpretation based on the roots of the most common Greek word *metanoia*. This is true, but it has the danger of being

1. D. Martyn Lloyd-Jones, *Revival*, (Westchester: Pickering and Inglis Ltd., 1987), 300

2. Watchman Nee, *Love Not the World*, (Fort Washington, Christian Literature Crusade, 1968), 91

incomplete, as if repentance were something casually intellectual. The Bible has a more full-orbed view. I see seven different qualities of true repentance: change of direction, sorrow, awareness, humility, active obedience, hope in Christ alone, and joy.

The primary Biblical texts for this study are Psalm 51 and Psalm 32. I would encourage you to take the time to read both of these psalms before continuing. David wrote them after he repented of both adultery and murder, and they give us a window into what real repentance looks like.

Change of Direction

In the Old Testament the most common word for repent (*naham*) takes on the meaning of *turning* from sin.

> "Repent and turn from all your transgressions, lest iniquity be your ruin. Cast away from you all the transgressions that you have committed, and make yourselves a new heart and a new spirit! Why will you die, O house of Israel? For I have no pleasure in the death of anyone, declares the Lord GOD; so turn, and live." (Ezekiel. 18:30–32)

In this verse repentance includes "casting away" and "turning away" from sin. You've had your moment of conviction by the Holy Spirit, you've seen the direction your life is heading, and by the grace of God you realize that you're going the wrong way. It's time for a course correction. God calls us to repent so that we may live. He doesn't want to see sin ruin your life; he wants to give you life.

This change of direction means that you will set aside old habits, such as casually surfing the Internet as you seek out suggestive material to amuse and arouse yourself, R-rated movies, photo sites, or having lots of time alone at home: these may be the beginnings of ensnarement, and you freely decide to avoid them. What you choose to avoid may be different from another person, but if you know yourself, you'll know where you are weak and where temptation is strong.

It also means that you will pursue new habits that bring you closer to God and give life. You'll apply yourself to God's word, prayer and fellowship. This is what Paul means in 2 Tim 2:22, "So *flee* youthful passions and *pursue* righteousness, faith, love, and peace, along with those who call on the Lord from a pure heart."

Setting aside those old habits and new temptations requires a firm commitment on your part. You must decide that you are not going to follow a course of life that leads to lust, and instead decide that you are going to follow a course of life that leads you to God and his blessings.

Sorrow

When a Christian becomes aware of his sin he feels remorse and deep sorrow. Modern psychology—as well as many Christians—will tell you that you shouldn't have these feelings at all, that it is wrong or legalistic to be sorry for your sins. This advice is misguided. You are sinning against God, yourself, and others when you look at pornography or enter into other sexual sin. You are objectifying God's daughters with your eyes and living for selfish satisfaction. The Holy Spirit will convict your heart over this, and you should feel sorrow over it. We see plenty of evidence of grief over sin in the writings of the Bible's authors.

"For when I kept silent, my bones wasted away through my groaning all day long. For day and night your hand was heavy upon me; my strength was dried up as by the heat of summer." (Psalm 32:3–4)

If you never feel a sense of sorrow, there could be something wrong, but feeling sorrow isn't enough; what is more important is where that sorrow leads. "For the sorrow that is according to the will of God produces a repentance without regret, leading to salvation, but the sorrow of the world produces death." (2 Corinthians 7:10) A true godly sorrow leads us to repent, because we know that we have grieved God. Paul describes two kinds of sorrow here: the sorrow that leads to repentance, and the sorrow that leads to death.

The sorrow that leads to death is called regret. Regret is sorrow for ourselves, sorrow that is pointed inward. There are two fruits of regret — the first is self-loathing. When Judas betrayed Christ for 30 pieces of silver, he "felt regret" and went and hanged himself. When we face our own sin we feel bad too. It is easy to take the self-destructive route. For you, that might be to allow yourself to spiral down into more sin, spending more time with porn, or adding new thrills like strip clubs, massage parlors, prostitutes, anonymous affairs with strangers, and so forth. In this kind of regret the cycle of failure, guilt, and shame is unbroken.

Another response to feelings of regret is to try to pay God back with good works. This response is all wrong too. In fact, in some ways it's worse because it allows us to keep up our appearance as good men, and ignores the grace of God. John Piper had this to say in one of his talks on sexual immorality:

> "If, by some means you get rid of lustful thoughts and slavery to pornography and fornication and adultery - without any reference to the knowledge of God, he won't get any glory for your new behavior. In other words, God is not just interested in what you do with your body, he is interested in — he is passionately concerned with — why you do it. If there is no connection between your knowing God, and your sexual purity, God gets no glory and you are in the grip of another idol."[3]

What then is the good kind of sorrow, the one that leads to repentance? Simply put, it is the sorrow that does not focus on how my sin affects me, but on how it affects God and others. It's sorrow without excuses and rationalizations. It's sorrow that faces the facts.

Awareness

When we repent there is an *awareness* of our fallen state, our weakness against temptation, and our hard-wired propensity toward rebellion. "For I recognize my rebellion; it haunts me day and night." (Psalm 51:3) "For I was born a sinner— yes, from the moment my mother conceived me." (Psalm 51:5) "And I know that nothing good lives in me, that is, in my sinful nature." (Romans 7:18) "The trouble is with me, for I am all too human, a

---

3. John Piper - "This is the Will of God for You: That You Abstain from Sexual Immorality", from www.desiringgod.org

slave to sin." (Romans 7:14, NLT) As you can see, David and Paul are both facing the facts: "I'm a sinner!"

We should not be surprised when we sin; that only shows that we don't really understand ourselves. True repentance requires self-awareness. The Puritan author John Owen put it this way: "Labor to know your own frame and temper; what spirit you are of; what associates in your heart Satan has; where corruption is strong, where grace is weak; what stronghold lust has in your natural constitution."[4] Pornography could be one of those associates that Satan has in your heart, a liaison with him, a harbinger of failure and shame. When you repent you acknowledge to God that stronghold within you, leaning on God's mercy, and you receive the grace of Christ as the only payment for it.

Repentance is also an awareness that our offense is primarily against God. "Against you, you only, have I sinned and done what is evil in your sight." (Psalm 51:4) David, the king of Israel, committed the sins of adultery, murder, lying, and political corruption when he took Bathsheba and killed her husband to cover it up. It would have been pretty hard to find anyone in Israel that David *didn't* sin against. Yet these words acknowledge that, ultimately, his sin was against God.

When you get into porn or other sexual sin, you are saying to God: "your plan for my sexuality is inadequate, your concern for the people I'm using for my pleasure is unwarranted, and your leadership over my life is an intrusion into my right of self-direction." We are in that

---

4. John Owen, *Temptation*, from Works vol. 6

moment refusing to honor God as God and the rightful ruler of our lives. Though you are certainly sinning against others, the primary sin is against God.

Humility

> "For you will not delight in sacrifice, or I would give it; you will not be pleased with a burnt offering. The sacrifices of God are a broken spirit; a broken and contrite heart, O God, you will not despise."(Psalm 51:16-17)

Humility strips away our self-sufficiency and puts us in touch with our need for the grace of God. It's only when we've given up on ourselves as the solution that we can draw near to God as the only provision. This is probably how David felt, too. "If there were something I could do about it, I would, but I've realized how useless that would be, and come to you with nothing but a heart that is broken, knowing that you love to give strength to the weak." David recognized that attempting to placate God by doing good works would only give him something to be proud of. More than that, it was important for his brokenness to be made public. He wrote a song about it, and we're still reading it after 3000 years.

It's entirely possible to be sorry for our sins without having humility. We are not really repentant if our self-sufficiency remains intact. Perhaps the best place to see our true humility before God is that we begin to practice it before men. All the posturing and deflections, all the pretending that everything is all right gets put away, and we appear before men as we really are, out of options other than the love and forgiveness of God and the cleansing blood of Christ. If you're reading this with a study group, you have an opportunity to practice this kind of humility. You can start allowing others to see your brokenness, and receive grace, comfort, and healing (James 5:16).

Active Obedience

If repentance involves a change of direction, you need to turn towards God when you turn away from sin, and live in the power of the new nature he has given you.

"Put to death therefore what is earthly in you: sexual immorality, impurity, passion, evil desire, and covetousness, which is idolatry. On account of these the wrath of God is coming. In these you too once walked, when you were living in them. But now you must put them all away: anger, wrath, malice, slander, and obscene talk from your mouth. Do not lie to one another, seeing that you have put off the old self with its practices and have put on the new self, which is being renewed in knowledge after the image of its creator." (Colossians 3:5-10)

Active obedience involves setting some things aside, such as immorality and greed, as well as putting on our new identity. Paul tells us to "put on the new self" — start living out of your identity in Christ! Get going with your walk with God! Don't stop moving forward! If you apply yourself to walking in the Spirit, you won't find the time, energy or inclination to apply yourself to fleshly lust (my personal paraphrase of Galatians 5:16). You will be finding fulfillment in following the leadership of your loving Father in heaven. Leave the past at the cross and follow.

John the Baptist told the religious pretenders of his
day how to recognize the reality of their faith: "Therefore
bear fruit in keeping with repentance" (Matthew 3:8) He
called on his listeners to live lives that were in harmony
with what they said they believed. Living out of our new
identity in Christ is real work: it takes courage, and grit,
and struggle. I think Paul had this in mind when he told
Timothy to "train yourself for godliness." (1 Timothy 4:7)
Like an athlete in training, we have to be disciplined in
godly living. But this effort and striving must always be
by grace, always in the power of the Holy Spirit. Paul
puts this beautifully in 1 Corinthians 15:10, "I worked
harder than any of them, though it was not I, but the
grace of God that is with me." Wherever we find a call
from the New Testament to obey God and his law of love,
it is based on the finished work of Christ on our behalf,
motivated by love for Jesus, and empowered by the Spirit.

The evidence of your repentance will be seen in the
choices you make. When presented with an opportunity
to sin, you have a choice: you can click on that link and
indulge your sinful nature, or you can choose to move off
that page, or close the browser. Each choice represents
an opportunity for failure or victory. It is in these small
moments of life that you are deciding what kind of person you are, and whom you want to follow. Every time
you decide to follow God's will in this matter, you are
bringing glory to him and choosing to live consistently
with who he says you are.

Hope in Christ Alone

> *For my pardon, this I see,*
> *nothing but the blood of Jesus;*
> *For my cleansing this my plea,*
> *nothing but the blood of Jesus.*
> Nothing But the Blood - Robert Lowery

In repenting we turn away from selfish lust, and turn toward grace-centered holiness. However, to do so in the power of the flesh is to return to sin—the sin of self-righteousness. The cross is the source of the Christian life, as Paul said, "… far be it from me to boast except in the cross of our Lord Jesus Christ." (Gal 6:14)

Our repentance can be so self-seeking ("If only I had a wife"), self-pitying ("Poor me, I'll never do any better"), and self-justifying ("I was tempted by that girl in my class"). One reason repentance is often half-hearted is that we feel bad, or feel sorry for ourselves, while at the same time we are justifying ourselves and blaming others for our failures. When we have truly repented before God, with a clear understanding of his holiness and our helplessness, we have finally come to the end of ourselves. No more excuses — I'm guilty as charged.

At that point we dare not allow ourselves to trust in anything but the finished work of Christ on our behalf. We see that we have no answers within, and look to the one who not only died, but also rose from the dead to victory over sin and death, and who intercedes for us, representing us before the Father. "For if while we were enemies we were reconciled to God by the death of his

Son, much more, now that we are reconciled, shall we
be saved by his life. " (Romans 5:10)

> "Yes, we must pursue obedience, but that obedience
> must always be cruciform, formed by Christ's cross.
> We must seek to obey because of the cross, find the
> grace to obey because of the cross, and live free
> from condemnation whether we succeed or fail in
> the light of the cross. The cross must be our only
> story, as Paul boldly proclaimed: 'For I decided to
> know nothing among you except Jesus Christ and
> him crucified' (1 Corinthians 2:2)."[5]

Joy

Lastly, repentance should be marked by something
that only God could bring from it: *Joy*. True repentance
is joyous because it looks beyond our condition as sinners
to the loving Father who has erased the debt. We rejoice
in repenting, not because we were let off the hook, but
because we are loved, not because we got pardoned, but
because we got Jesus.

Look at David's reaction when he sees past the pain
to God: "Let me hear joy and gladness; let the bones
that you have broken rejoice." (Psalm 51:8) "Deliver me
from bloodguilt, O God, O God of my salvation, and my
tongue will sing aloud of your righteousness. O Lord,
open my lips, and my mouth will declare your praise."
(Psalm 51:14-15) See also how his joy is dependent on
God. He wants God to be the foundation of his joy and
to energize it.

---

5. Elyse Fitzpatrick and Dennis Johnson, *Counsel from the Cross*
(Wheaton, Ill.: Crossway Books, 2009) 171-172

Psalm 32 begins with joy: "Blessed is the one whose transgression is forgiven, whose sin is covered. Blessed is the man against whom the LORD counts no iniquity, and in whose spirit there is no deceit." (Psalm 32:1–2)

Of course you should rejoice! God rejoices when we repent of our sins: "There will be more joy in heaven over one sinner who repents than over ninety-nine righteous persons who need no repentance." (Luke 15:7) Repentance brings us back to the ever-welcoming arms of our Father in heaven. Take a look at Luke 15: there are three stories there: the lost sheep, the lost coin, and the lost or "prodigal" son. In each story, the main subject is the joy of the one who finds what is lost. In repentance you align your joy with the loving Father.

Conclusion

So, what of our initial claim that "all of life is repentance"? Is repentance something that is a lifelong process? Even though we have salvation, we stand before a holy and righteous God stained with indwelling sin. In order to apply the grace of God to our guilty consciences, we must acknowledge that sin before Him, and immediately claim the power of the blood of Christ.

If our sin takes us far from God, it should follow that repentance brings us closer to Him. This is what we were created for: relationship with God and fellowship with Him. The point of repentance for the Christian is not just to feel better — if you really see it that way you are missing the point entirely — the point of repentance is to be near to God again, to restore that fellowship.

You will find as you progress in faith that repentance will enter into a deeper, wider arena. You may stop looking at porn but find yourself having persistent sexual fantasies, or notice that you constantly check out women's bodies as you walk down the street. Those fantasies or that second look will be things you must bring to God as well, as the Spirit convicts you of them. He will reveal many other sins in thought, word, and deed for which you must repent. In truth, you will never come to the end of this need to be cleansed on a daily basis.

According to John Murray:

> "Christ's blood is the laver of initial cleansing, but it is also the fountain to which the believer must continuously repair. It is at the cross of Christ that repentance has its beginning; it is at the cross of Christ that it must continue to pour out its heart in the tears of confession and contrition for the sin of the past and of the present."[6]

Many times the conviction of the Holy Spirit comes to us as that quiet voice in our hearts, or from other people, but I find that most often that conviction comes from God's word. As the truth of God found in the pages of the Bible changes our thinking, renewing our minds, we become aware of our need for repentance. There's nothing better than seeing the direction God has for our lives to realize that our own path has taken us off course. In the next chapter we're going to study how the Word of God transforms and renews our hearts.

---

6. John Murray, *Redemption Accomplished and Applied*, (Grand Rapids, MI: Eerdmans, 1955) 116

For group discussion

Talk about your experience since you last met. Confess your sins to each other, focusing on how God has convicted you of them through the Holy Spirit.

Have you ever repented in a way that was self-pitying or self-justifying? What kind of thoughts did you have during this kind of "sorrow that leads to death"? In what ways does repentance differ from simply regret for you?

Have you ever repented in a way that was without self-pity, or pride, where you were honest, humble, and trusting in God's provision? What was that process like? What were the effects?

Pray for each member in your group, acknowledging your sinfulness and thanking him for the standing that you have in grace through Christ. Pray for strength for those who are seeking repentance from the heart.

Six

A Mind Renewed

In 1964, almost 30 years before the first graphical web browser, Marshall McLuhan coined the phrase "the medium is the message." One of the things that he meant by this was: if you evaluate any form of media solely based on its content, you're missing part of the message. The Internet and the World Wide Web have proven him right. Fast forward to the present, where people are connected in one way or another to a flood of information via cell phones, iPhones, Androids, iPads, Blackberrys, netbooks, laptops, desktops and more. The Internet has changed the way we read, shop, and even talk to one another.

The Internet has a vast array of resources and information, but no resource on the Internet is more available and pervasive than pornography. If all media has a message, what is the message of porn? Does Internet pornography merely arouse and entertain, or does it carry with it a message, one which instructs us, even trains us? Pornography teaches us that sex is about the physical, that sex is divorced from relationships, that people are objects to be used to achieve pleasure. Pornography teaches us that as long as pleasure is achieved, there are no boundaries.

There is a principle that runs throughout the entire Bible – we reflect that which we behold. When Moses beheld the glory of God, his face shone in reflection of that glory (Exodus 34:29-30). As we noted in chapter 2, Psalm 115 tells us that those who practice idolatry will become like the ones they worship, blinded to the truth, and deaf to the voice of God, in the same way that the statues they are bowing down to are blind and deaf. In 2 Corinthians 3:18 Paul says, "And we all, with unveiled face beholding the glory of the Lord, are being transformed into the same image from one degree of glory to another." To behold the glory of God is to be transformed by it.

Paul says in Romans 1 that those who did not honor God "exchanged the glory of the Lord for an image", that they "exchanged the truth of God for a lie", and then exchanged their natural sexuality for that which is unnatural. Whatever we exchange God for, we also reflect. If we watch pornography, we will inevitably reflect the message of porn, the message of the world system, the message of our enemy, Satan. We choose what we *behold* and in turn then, *reflect* what we behold. Those choices are then reflected in how we think.

The thought life is where our daily battle is, where sin captivates us, but also where truth liberates us. All sexual behavior starts first as sexual desire in the mind. In the first chapter we discussed the negative effects of pornography on the mind: how looking at porn "trains" us to see women as objects, inhibits our ability to have intimacy, and diminishes our capacity to enjoy normal sex.

The person who uses pornography finds that it overlays his normal thinking, creating a virtual fantasy world that affects everyday life and relationships all the while masking its negative effects from the thinking brain. Men who regularly look at porn don't think that there's anything wrong, but while the mind is being distorted, all around them their lives and relationships deteriorate.

In chapter 3 we talked about the cycle of addiction: preoccupation, ritualization, sexual compulsivity, and shame and despair. Once that cycle has been entered, it is very difficult to break. The first part, preoccupation, is the point at which the battle for your mind begins. What you do with your mind on a daily basis directly affects the outcome of that inner conflict. If your mind is not being instructed and renewed by the word of God on a daily basis, you will more easily give in to temptation. As you lose these skirmishes against lust, you also lose your taste for God's truth, and slowly begin to forget his perspective. The world, flesh, and the devil are always insidiously working, trying to "train" us in selfishness.

A mind renewed

Because of these things, the first important step that you must take to find restoration is to have your mind renewed. If years of looking at porn have affected how you think and view the world around you, then you need to get your mind fixed; all you need is some mental renewal. Does that sound too easy? That is exactly what God is willing to do for you.

> "Don't be conformed to this world, but be transformed by the renewing of your mind, so that you may prove what the will of God is, that which is good, acceptable, and perfect." (Romans 12:2)

In our context, "being conformed to this world" is precisely the kind of internal damage that we face. The perspective of "this world" is woven into the fabric of pornography. Ideas like "I must have my needs met," "what's wrong with a little self-gratification," "the physical is all that matters," "women like it rough," "no means yes," and other messages found in pornography all have their origin in what the Bible calls the *kosmos*, the world system directed by God's enemy Satan.[1] These values and principles are echoed elsewhere; we see them in business, advertising, the university classroom, and especially in all forms of modern media. The underlying philosophy of the *kosmos* is to reject God's right to rule and elevate the desires of self at the expense of all else.

When Paul says, "don't be conformed" to these ideas, the Greek verb is in the passive voice, meaning that conformity is something that happens *to* us. As we listen to the song of the world system, especially through pornography, we are unwittingly changed; we reflect what we behold. We didn't decide to be conformed. Nonetheless, seeking after lust and self first will have its price, the price of conformity to the values of the world.

Instead of being conformed, Paul urges us to "be transformed." This is also spoken in the passive voice; it's also something that happens to us. This transformation is a direct work of the Spirit of God; he can renew your mind and restore your thinking to wholeness. There is only one way that we can be renewed in this way, and that is through the agency of the Word of God, the Bible itself. In order to resist the influence of the prevailing views of this evil world, you have to think the thoughts

1. For more on the Biblical understanding of the kosmos, see chapter 11, Dennis McCallum, *Satan and His Kingdom: What the Bible Says and How It Matters to You*, (Bethany House, 2009), and Watchman Nee, *Love Not the World*, (CLC Publications, 2004).

of God. Romans 12:2 speaks of no third alternative: you are either being conformed to the beliefs of this world or you're allowing God to transform you. That transformation comes from his truth.

The Power of the Word

> "All Scripture is breathed out by God and profitable for teaching, for reproof, for correction, and for training in righteousness, that the man of God may be competent, equipped for every good work." (2 Timothy 3:16-17)

All Scripture is "breathed out by God" – he has spoken to us! We have true revelation from him that touches every part of our lives! The Greek word, *theopneustos*, communicates the fact that God spoke through the agency of the Holy Spirit, breathing his truth into men who wrote the books of the Bible. The allusion to God's breathing life into Adam (Genesis 2:7) should not be missed. When God breathed the breath of life into Adam, he became a living being. To us as well, God's word is life, just as Jesus said: "The words that I have spoken to you are spirit and life." (John 6:63)

There is power in the word of God. The universe was created when God spoke it into existence, and the refrain of "He spoke... and it was" continues throughout Genesis 1. When Satan decided to tempt Adam and Eve, it was God's word that he assaulted – "did God really say?" God revealed his Law to Moses through words, spoke to the people through the words of prophets, and finally spoke to us in his Son (Hebrews 1:1-2).

In his gospel, John introduces Jesus as the Word, the final expression that brings life through light (John 1:1-4). Jesus came with a message: that the kingdom of God had come in his person, and his charge to the disciples before returning to his Father was to take the message of good news to all peoples, tribes, and nations. God's word, wherever we find it, is powerful, able to create a universe, able to raise the dead (John 11:43), able to still violent storms (Mark 4:39), able to heal (Matthew 8:8), and able to bring us to salvation (Romans 10:17).

Stop and think for a moment: is the word of God powerful enough to create new desires in your heart, to raise you to walking in new life, to still the storm of lust in your heart, to heal the damage of sexual sin, and to bring you into the joy of your salvation? You have God's promise that it can. His Word is that powerful.

According to 2 Timothy 3:16 the Word is profitable, or useful to us. The Word teaches us, corrects wrong thinking and behavior, and trains us in righteousness. In order for those things to happen you must spend time with God in His word, reading, studying, meditating on it, and following it in obedience. You need to become absorbed in the Word of God.

Becoming Absorbed in God's Word

Robert Benchley, the humorist writer for the New Yorker is known for saying that "there are two kinds of people in the world: those who divide the world into two kinds of people, and those who don't." The Bible affirms that there are really only two kinds of people: the righteous and the wicked. This psalm contrasts both of them:

1- Blessed is the man who does not walk in the counsel of the wicked or stand in the way of sinners or sit in the seat of mockers.

2- But his delight is in the law of the Lord, and on his law he meditates day and night.

3- He is like a tree planted by streams of water, which yields its fruit in season and whose leaf does not wither. Whatever he does prospers." (Psalm 1:1-3)

In verse 1 there is a progression from walking to standing to finally sitting. At first, the person is just rubbing shoulders with those who are going their own way instead of God's. They have associations with the "counsel of the wicked", the thinking of this world system, the reigning philosophy of our day. If they follow that course long enough, they may find themselves "standing in the way of sinners." To "stand in the way" of sinners does not mean to oppose them, but to stand in their shoes. He has gone from entertaining the ideas of the wicked to trying them on for size. Increasingly, he adopts the lifestyle and ways of thinking of those who are not following God. Finally, he sits down in the seat of mockers. He is in the recliner with his feet up, and the remote at the ready. At this point, wickedness is so entrenched that he sits down, ready to mock everyone and everything, and especially those who are living for God.

What does the godly person look like? "But his delight is in the law of the Lord, and on his law he meditates day and night."

There is an interesting contrast here: it doesn't really say how he walks, stands, or sits, but instead tells us what he delights in and thinks about. He is deeply influenced by the teaching of the Lord, and this orientation defines him. The righteous man doesn't just read God's word in a daily 5 minutes of "devotion"; he lets it become an integral part of his thinking. As a result, there is not a time in his day that is not affected by God's thoughts. More than this, he delights in it; it brings him joy. It's a heart attitude, a direction.

The effect of this orientation in the godly person's life is given in verse 3:

> "He is like a tree planted by streams of water, which yields its fruit in season and whose leaf does not wither. Whatever he does, prospers."

This is not just a tree that sprang up somewhere; it's planted. The Hebrew idiom used here indicates a conscious choice of location. You want your life to be intentional, not just carried along by the winds blowing through the *kosmos*. In Palestine if you wanted a tree to survive you would plant it near water. This verse refers to streams (plural) of water, a confluence of water. The word picture of fruit and leaf is one of vitality, ending with the summary statement – whatever he does prospers.

This idea of prospering as a result of an orientation toward the word of God echoes what God told Joshua:

> "This Book of the Law shall not depart from your mouth, but you shall meditate on it day and night, so that you may be careful to do according to all that is written in it. For then you will make your

way prosperous, and then you will have good success." (Joshua 1:8)

We see the same idea emphasized in Romans 12:2 – "that you may prove what the will of God is, that which is good, acceptable and perfect." Our lives stop being a reflection of the conforming work of the world's attitudes and start to reflect the will of God.

As followers of Jesus, we have a choice: we can either be influenced by the *kosmos* or by God's truth. Our commitment to that choice will be evident in how much time we devote to the word of God and our attitude towards his truth. Your attitude is extremely important - you can spend 12 hours a day reading the Bible, and not be transformed. The Psalmist's devotion was combined with delight. He knew the answers were there for him, and he rejoiced in finding them.

This choice is an either/or situation: you will either pursue mental transformation through God's word and have your mind renewed, or the world with its relentless message of selfishness will "squeeze you into its mold."

In his psalm about the word of God, David has some sound wisdom for those seeking purity:

"How can a young man stay pure? By obeying your word. I have tried hard to find you— don't let me wander from your commands. I have hidden your word in my heart, that I might not sin against you. I praise you, O Lord; teach me your decrees. I have recited aloud all the regulations you have given us. I have rejoiced in your laws as much as in riches. I will study your commandments and reflect on your ways. I will delight in your decrees and not forget your word." (Psalm 119:9-16)

David's goal is to obey the word of the Lord, and although obedience may not be the starting point of that journey, he explains how to get there: "I have hidden your word in my heart." In order to prepare for temptation you need to know what God says, to have his perspective clearly before you. You probably will not have your Bible open in front of you when you are tempted to stray from your convictions about sexual purity, so instead it needs to saturate your thinking enough so that spiritual truth comes to your mind frequently.

This means that you are going to have to memorize scripture. Maybe memorizing the Bible seems archaic, like spinning wool into thread, or churning butter, but memorizing the Bible is easy when it's your delight, like David — "I have rejoiced in your laws as much as in riches," "I delight in your decrees." How do we learn to delight in the word of the Lord? I think there are a lot of ways to get a taste for the word of God, such as listening to good teaching or reading good books, but most of all, I think we begin to delight in the word of God as we see his power affecting our lives through revealed truth. When you've read, studied, meditated on, and applied it to your life, and you've seen God working as a result, it's exciting! At some point you have to decide that you want to do this for yourself and make the time in your life to read, study, reflect and memorize. As God more and more becomes your delight, so too does His word.

Identity Thinking

What we believe about ourselves drives the choices we make, and ultimately the person we choose to be. If you think of yourself as basically a worthless person, you might end up fulfilling that self-imposed destiny. If instead, you see yourself as better than everyone else, that will affect how you relate to others. When you consider what the Bible says is true of you as a Christian, you'll discover an amazing contrast with what we typically think of ourselves.

The important thing is this: who we are in our natural condition is not what matters; it's who you are in Christ! When you study your Bible, you should be looking for truths that speak of your identity in Christ. Take a passage like Ephesians 1:3-14, for example. There we discover the following things that are true of you because you are in Christ:

- You are blessed in Christ with every spiritual blessing in the heavenly places.
- You were chosen in him before the foundation of the world.
- You were predestined to adoption as sons.
- You have redemption through his blood.
- You have the forgiveness of your trespasses.
- You have his grace lavished upon you.
- You have access to the knowledge of the mystery of his will.
- You have a unique role in God's purpose in history.
- You have obtained an inheritance.

- You will be to the praise of his glory.
- You were sealed with the promised Holy Spirit.

If you have fallen into the trap of pornography as a Christian, you have lost sight of who you really are in Christ. You're still thinking like a slave to sin. You're still thinking like an orphan, and not the adopted son of your Father in heaven. Understanding who you really are will change your attitude about sexual sin, not by making you feel bad about it, but by making you grateful for the new identity that you have received.

That's why Paul encourages us:

> "If then you have been raised with Christ, seek the things that are above, where Christ is, seated at the right hand of God. *Set your minds on things that are above, not on things that are on earth.* For you have died, and your life is hidden with Christ in God." (Colossians 3:1-3, italics mine)

Setting your mind on the things above means that you believe what God says about who you are, regardless of what you see in your day–to–day behavior. So does that mean that our behavior doesn't really matter? Not at all! The word of God transforms our thinking, and the Holy Spirit enables us to obey the word of God.

Obedience to the Word

> "Do not merely listen to the word, and so deceive yourselves. Do what it says. Anyone who listens to the word but does not do what it says is like a man who looks at his face in a mirror and, after looking at himself, goes away and immediately forgets

what he looks like. But the man who looks intently into the perfect law that gives freedom, and continues to do this, not forgetting what he has heard, but doing it—he will be blessed in what he does." (James 1:22-25)

This last point is a critical reminder: we must connect the word of God to our life; we must do what it says. Many of us who study the Bible do so functionally, but often have little experience of its transforming power in our lives, not because we are not orthodox in our understanding, but having understood what it says we are not willing to put it into practice.

James says it's like looking in a mirror: your face is dirty, your hair is a mess, and you need a shave. If you got up in the morning and did that, and then proceeded on to work or school, what was the point of looking in the mirror? The mirror did its work in showing you what you needed to do, but you went on your way as if you had been shown nothing at all. Jesus also warned us against hearing without action:

"Why do you call me 'Lord, Lord,' and not do what I tell you? Everyone who comes to me and hears my words and does them, I will show you what he is like: he is like a man building a house, who dug deep and laid the foundation on the rock. And when a flood arose, the stream broke against that house and could not shake it, because it had been well built. But the one who hears and does not do them is like a man who built a house on the ground without a foundation. When the stream broke against it, immediately it fell, and the ruin of that house was great." (Luke 6:46-49)

There is both a warning and a promise here: those who hear what God has to say but ignore it are setting themselves up for ruin. Those, however, who act on what the word of God says, have a solid foundation for their lives.

Practical Steps

You can decide that you're not going to look at porn any more, but if your thinking is still fundamentally flawed, you will probably fail in your resolve. Engaging in a rigorous program of mental transformation is critical to your success. You must become absorbed in the word of God. Martin Luther once said,

> "In truth, you cannot read too much in Scripture, and what you read, you cannot read too carefully, and what you read carefully, you cannot understand too well, and what you understand well, you cannot teach too well, and what you teach well, you cannot live too well. The devil, the world and our flesh are raging and raving against us... this evil, shameful time is not the season for being lazy, for sleeping and snoring."[2]

A regular program of studying and memorizing the Word of God is a huge part of how we resist the grip of sin in our lives. If you have never really undertaken a serious study of the Bible before, you might be uncertain

2. Martin Luther, quoted from McKim, Donald K, *The Cambridge companion to Martin Luther*. (Cambridge University Press, 2003), 141

how to proceed. There are many ways to study God's word and a variety of systems for reading and studying the Bible. Here are a few guidelines that might help you:

1. *Find time in the Word every day.* Reading the Bible daily is an essential component to cultivating a spiritual perspective. Ideally, start your day with reading the Bible. This is the best way to put your mind in a frame that is focused on spiritual truth. If that's not possible for you, then whenever you can find consistent time in the Word of God will work. You have a need to feed daily on the word of God. (1 Peter 2:2)

2. *Prayerfully meditate on what you read.* Reading the Bible like it's a brief article in a newspaper or blog is not what we're talking about here. As you read, interact with God on what you're reading. Take the time to think about it, and ask questions of the text. Where is the main point? What did the author intend when he wrote it? What do you (God) want me to see here? When you encounter a difficult saying, or something you don't understand, ask God to reveal its meaning to you. Wrestle with the text in communion with God so that it gives up the nourishment that your soul needs. Keep a notebook, and make notes on what was revealed, what you saw for the first time, what was difficult.

3. *Look for identity truths.* When you see something that is true of you because you are in Christ, think about how your new identity should affect how you live. How does who you are in Christ affect you when you face criticism, disappointment, or challenges in relationships? How does who you are in Christ impact your job, your home, or your ministry?

4. *Look for the promises of God.* The promises of God give us an opportunity for exercising our faith. Plan how you will respond to what God promises. God makes big promises to us. We should not dabble in them, but dive in headfirst.

> It is the word of God alone which can first and effectually cheer the heart of any sinner. There is no true or solid peace to be enjoyed in the world except in the way of reposing upon the promises of God. Those who do not resort to them may succeed for a time in hushing or evading the terrors of conscience, but they must ever be strangers to true inward comfort.[3]

5. *Look for the cross.* The cross cuts across every word of Scripture. Though not every word in the Bible is about the cross, they all live in proximity to it, and serve to point us to it. When Jesus tells us to "love one another as I have loved you," we cannot but think of the cross as the ultimate demonstration and proof of his love. When Paul tells us to be "anxious for nothing," we can trust in God because Jesus faced his own anxiety in the garden of Gethsemane as he considered bearing our sin, and emerged victorious over fear on our behalf, and made peace between God and us by his sacrifice.

The word of God is powerful and gives life, and there is no other way to have your mind renewed than to dig deep into God's truth. Why not get started right now?

---

3. John Calvin, *Institutes, IV. 8. 8*

For group discussion:

Talk about how things have been going since you last met. Rejoice in one another's victories and show grace and understanding for one another's failures.

What types of things do you find yourself spending a lot of time thinking about? How much effect does your thought life have on your daily actions?

Talk about those times the Word of God has impacted you. Have you ever changed the direction of your life because of the Word? Tell us about it.

How can you connect the identity truths mentioned in this chapter to your fight against sexual sin?

Pray for each member in your group. Give thanks to God for the transforming power of his truth. Pray for the strength to obey his word in tough times.

SEVEN

LIVING IN THE LIGHT OF COMMUNITY

"Each time that I have a fall, I get hit immediately with lies from the Evil One and my own flesh which only wants to survive. Sometimes these voices win, and I enter into a chaotic pattern, but other times God pierces my soul and reminds me I am loved and accepted just the way I am. I confess to my Lord to remain hopeful that he will change me and heal this area of my life. I confess to my brothers in Christ because God calls us to bear our burdens with one another. I confess to my wife when it has impacted our marriage. She is not the sin police in my life, but I want her to be a part of this struggle so we can talk and pray together to remain unified in this fight.

God is gracious, but hates sin. He knows this more than I can ever comprehend, and that is why I must fall at the foot of the cross with each sin. Any stray of the mind needs to be brought to the Lord. Too often when I hear someone say, "Well, it wasn't hard core porn," I remind him that justifying a fall is a very dangerous game to play, one that Satan loves for us to sit in and for us to be happy about only toe dangling and searching without actually looking. Each stray for me needs to have a confession.

In the last chapter, we saw the importance of the word of God in renewing our minds from the damage that pornography causes. Equally important is the practice of regular confession before God and men. The word of God is the means of transformation by the Holy Spirit. Being open and honest with others makes the grace of God real to us and releases our hearts from the condemning grip of sin and guilt that silence has had on us.

If you want to find freedom from sexual sin, confession isn't just important – it's *necessary*. Personally, I have never seen anyone recover from sexual addiction that remained in silence.

Why don't we freely share our failures with one another? We usually don't want to confess our sins because we want to look good before men. We hold on to the persona that we have created so that others will think highly of us. In reality, that persona is often the very thing that blocks our spiritual growth. We need other people, but other people can't have much genuine effect if the person they are talking to is a sham.

The Christian life is meant to be lived in community. Never forget what that community is: it's a community of sinners who are totally dependent on the grace of God and the sacrifice of Christ for their righteousness; we need each other precisely *because* we are sinners.

> "For there is no distinction: for all have sinned and
> fall short of the glory of God, and are justified by
> his grace as a gift, through the redemption that is
> in Christ Jesus" (Romans 3:22-23).

Every one of us falls short, every one of us is justified purely by grace, and there is no point in any of us pretending that we can stand on our own before God.

The moment you decide that you're going to keep your last sexual escapade a secret, you are passing off a lie to others, and at the same time increasing your toleration of sin. Only when you confess your sin do you experience the healing power of the blood of Christ, "who cleanses us from all unrighteousness" (1 John 1:9).

Norman Grubb stresses this point in his excellent little book, *Continuous Revival:*

> "Though hardly realizing it, while we are careful to keep the roof off between ourselves and God through repentance and faith, we soon let those walls of respectability creep up again between ourselves and our brethren. We don't mind our brethren knowing about successes in our Christian living... because we too get a little reflected credit out of those things. But where we fail, in those many, many areas of our daily lives -- that is a different question! If God has to deal with us over our impatience or temper in the home, over dishonesty in our business, over coldness or other sins, by no means do we easily bear testimony to our brethren of God's faithful and gracious dealings in such areas of failure. Why not? Just because of pride, self-esteem, although we would often more conveniently call it reserve! The fact is we love the praise of men as well as of God, and that is exactly what the Scriptures say stops the flow of confession before men (John 12:42-43).[1]

---

1. Norman Grubb, *Continuous Revival*, (CLC Publications)

Mutual exhortation

The author of the book of Hebrews said, "But exhort one another every day, as long as it is called "today," that none of you may be hardened by the deceitfulness of sin" (Hebrews 3:13). Another word for "exhortation" would be "encouragement." This short passage teaches us three things that we need to apply in order to live openly with one another:

First, *our need is daily* – it's regular. All your sins, known and unknown to you, were paid for at the cross. Nonetheless, it is important to acknowledge our sins before God as we realize them, as well as be in relationships where we can confess our failures. "Whoever conceals his transgressions will not prosper, but he who confesses and forsakes them will obtain mercy" (Proverbs 28:13). When you stifle your confession before God and men, you may begin to think that you have "gotten away with it." As you tolerate sin, you also begin to lose sight of how damaging it is. "It's not really a big deal," you say. "If it happens again, maybe I'll talk to someone about it." When you procrastinate, delay becomes rationalization, and rationalization becomes justification. At that point you're caught in a sin trap.

Secondly, exhortation is *mutual*. We are to exhort *one another*. Some of us are spectators in life, and others play the role of experts. There is no place in the body of Christ for either. You may be a spectator: if you're in a small group or an accountability group, you sit and observe. The testimonies of others seem more important or more interesting than your own. Spectators either think their sins are not worth mentioning, or they feel "shy" about sharing their own struggles. This is usually just a veneer over the spectator's self-righteousness. A spectator will not reveal anything until pressed to do so in many cases. If you tend to be a spectator, it's important for you to practice openness with others.

The expert is another matter: experts tend to comment on everything, and reveal nothing. They always have an observation on what others say, or a word of knowledge on some topic, they can trot out interesting anecdotes about others' sins or their own past issues (rarely in the present), and so forth. They won't open up deeply and humbly. You might think the expert insightful, but not knowable. The expert is usually just another persona, and if you are one, those around you will either (wrongly) think that you don't have any struggles, or (probably rightly) think that you're just a liar.

If you're a spectator or an expert you will miss out on the sweetness of mutual fellowship and encouragement. You'll miss out on the healing that is available to you from the Holy Spirit through the agency of the body of Christ. God calls us to openness with both our struggles and victories in a context of mutual respect.

The third thing we learn from Hebrews 3:13 is that *sin deceives, and then hardens.* One of the reasons that God calls us into community is to protect us from the tendency to allow our sin to isolate and deceive us.

The more you remain silent about your sin before others, the more difficult it will become to see things clearly. Your heart will grow harder against God as well as the advice of others. Sin will begin its deadly silent process of reigning over you. You can tragically end up as the one described in Psalm 36:

> "Transgression speaks to the wicked deep in his
> heart; there is no fear of God before his eyes. For
> he flatters himself in his own eyes that his iniquity
> cannot be found out and hated. The words of his
> mouth are trouble and deceit; he has ceased to act
> wisely and do good. He plots trouble while on his
> bed; he sets himself in a way that is not good; he
> does not reject evil" (Psalm 36:1–4).

A Christian who admits his sin lives in integrity. You
demonstrate that you believe the truth of the gospel when
you live openly, honestly, and transparently. At the same
time, confession keeps us sensitive to the Holy Spirit's
transforming work, and allows God to show us a way
forward through the counsel of others. Having a mind
predisposed to that kind of dialogue with God and others opens the door for the Spirit to work on our hearts,
while allowing us and others to see the effect of that work.

Walking in the Light

> "But if we walk in the light, as he is in the light, we
> have fellowship with one another, and the blood of
> Jesus his Son cleanses us from all sin" (1 John 1:7).

What a beautiful picture this is of living opening in
community – walking in the light. We walk honestly
before others, knowing that there is nothing to hide,
nothing to gain, and nothing to lose. The Christian life is
not perfection — John would have said something like "if
we walk according to the light" if that were the case. Our
sin is here, but it's out in the open so we can experience

both fellowship and the cleansing of our consciences. Paul teaches the same thing in Ephesians:

> "Since you have heard about Jesus and have learned the truth that comes from him, throw off your old sinful nature and your former way of life, which is corrupted by lust and deception. Instead, let the Spirit renew your thoughts and attitudes. Put on your new nature, created to be like God—truly righteous and holy. So stop telling lies. Let us tell our neighbors the truth, for we are all parts of the same body" (Ephesians 4:21–25, NLT).

Notice how Paul ties honesty with the new nature, "let us tell our neighbors the truth, for we are all parts of the same body." We have learned the truth from Jesus about our status as adopted sons, members of one another, and we are renewed as we tell the truth about ourselves to our brothers. This is why God's word is so important in all this: we need to know the truth to "speak the truth in love" (Ephesians 4:15) to one another. Our honesty does not just come from our subjective feelings about ourselves — it's informed by the revelation we receive from the word of God.

> "For the word of God is living and active, sharper than any two-edged sword, piercing to the division of soul and of spirit, of joints and of marrow, and discerning the thoughts and intentions of the heart. And no creature is hidden from his sight, but all are naked and exposed to the eyes of him to whom we must give account" (Hebrews 4:12–13).

As we dig deeply into the word of God, we get revelation from God that moves past our actions down into the intentions of the heart. The quality of our confession improves as we begin to share not just what we have done, but also our enlightened understanding of *why* we did it. There is a real difference between telling a brother, "I got into porn last night" and telling him, "I was really angry after that conversation yesterday afternoon, and I felt entitled to get into porn last night."

There will come a day when we will all give an account to God for how we have lived our lives. This will be a comprehensive evaluation with a full disclosure of our deeds and motives, and the Bible teaches that it will be done in public (1 Corinthians 3:10-15). God will not only reveal our deeds, but also the motives and intentions of our hearts behind those deeds, "who will bring to light the things now hidden in darkness and will disclose the purposes of the heart. Then each one will receive his commendation from God" (1 Corinthians 4:5).

Will everyone you know be surprised at what they learn there about you? If today you posture before others as the righteous person you are not, it won't change the disclosure in heaven. However, if you want to experience God's grace right now there is nothing better for it than to open up to others about what's really going on in your life. The Bible promises that we are healed when we openly confess our sins to each other.

What is Accountability?

> "Therefore, confess your sins to one another and pray for one another, that you may be healed. The prayer of a righteous person has great power as it is working" (James 5:16).

It wouldn't be appropriate to tell everyone you know about your deepest sins; you need to have someone in your life that you can tell anything to, someone who will pray for you and encourage you. If you're reading this with a group of men then you have the basis for just such a relationship. Most people call this kind of person an *accountability partner*, but that's a term that needs some definition.

Accountability is not about being a *police officer*; you aren't trying to catch someone sinning. I prefer to think of an accountability partner as someone with an *informed curiosity*. He knows where you are weak (hopefully because you told him), and he asks questions to see how you are doing in multiple areas of your life. Your sexual sin is hard to talk about. There is the shame and embarrassment of failure, the desire to look good in the eyes of others, and the tendency to minimize what is really going on. A good accountability partner will find that understandable, but shouldn't accept indirect, vague answers to probing questions. Things like "my week's been pretty good" or "I think I've been doing well lately" are likely to be nothing more than misdirection. His questions need to be specific enough so that, if you're going to lie, you'll have to do so directly. You should make a prior agreement that you are both going to be specific about what's been going on.

If pornography is your issue, questions like "How many times? How long? What kind of material?" should be agreed upon as appropriate. This needs to be a person you feel safe talking with. You may widen your circle of accountability in time, but one good reliable friend is the best starting point.

Accountability is not about *playing the role of the person's conscience*, or making sure the person is unable to make a mistake. I have had a number of people ask me to "hold them accountable" for one thing or another over the years. This often amounts to them asking me to play the role of making sure they don't step out of line, or being their conscience for them. An accountability partner leaves the Holy Spirit room to do his work in the heart of the other person.

Accountability is not about *pornography alone*. Your accountability partner should also be taking an interest in other areas of your spiritual growth, or other difficulties you might be encountering. The Christian life is not about avoiding sin, but about faith working through love. If you went the rest of your life without ever sinning sexually, but never grew in "all aspects unto Him who is the head, even Christ", what would it profit you? You could end up a chaste Pharisee, a mean judgmental little man with no real virtues, and not a friend in the world. The goal of accountability is for you to build intimate relationships with others, to live a full, rich life of faith and joy in the Holy Spirit, while carrying out the mission of spreading the gospel and building up the body of Christ.

Choosing an Accountability Partner

You should be selective about accountability partners; there are some people who do not make good ones.

If you're married, your wife is someone whose trust you need to earn, and you must be honest with her about your struggle, but that is different than having her checking on you, or reporting to her every time you get into sin. This will cause her a great deal of pain unless she is very mature. My experience is that most men won't be that honest in order to spare her feelings, or to keep peace in the home, and you will probably lie and minimize your sin. I know that this is a controversial point, but my experience with men who "report in" to their wives is that they often hurt them deeply as they report every fall, every thought, and every stray look. Their wives become afraid of their possible infidelity to her, and that fear leads to control. Your wife needs your full disclosure of your problem, but she also needs to trust in the Holy Spirit and the men God has placed in your life.

You do not want someone who is compromised in this area for an accountability partner. A person who is losing the battle against lust might not feel much conviction about your problem, since it could possibly expose his own issues.

On the other hand, neither do you want someone who can't understand why anyone would have a problem in this area. There are those guys, for instance, who can't understand why anyone would look at porn. These men are getting harder to find, but they're out there, and you may encounter nothing more than a judgmental, critical spirit instead of truth telling and compassion.

Lastly you do not want someone as an accountability partner who is very passive in relating. We all know men that will not press us for more information, or be willing to be forceful or direct when the situation requires it. This is the kind of guy that our sin nature wants, but if we're going to grow we want men who will speak truth into our lives. A passive man is often too concerned with his own inner life to take enough interest in the life of another, much less take the kind of steps that might lead to confrontation. You are looking for a man who will see through your smoke screen and persist with you. You want a manly man who will love you enough to call you out when you're sidestepping the conviction of God.

Accountability Software

One thing that has made a huge difference in my life and the lives of others is accountability software. Accountability software is not a porn blocker: it's a program that sends a report of your Internet activity to your accountability partner or partners. If you go to a questionable web site, your friend is going to know about it, and the two of you have the opportunity for a conversation. Regardless of whatever other Internet solutions you use, I consider accountability software to be essential. If your partner is not going to read it, it won't do much good. Do not send it to the guy who never reads his email.

Though I am not affiliated personally with them, I consider Covenant Eyes to be the best Internet accountability solution.[2] Their software is the best quality I have found. It has excellent scoring and reporting. It's much

---

2. www.covenanteyes.com

harder to circumvent than other solutions, especially the free ones. Covenant Eyes also has a filter offering for those who are looking for an Internet filter.

I get asked all the time about porn blockers. If you have children, I consider porn blocking software to be essential on any computer they have access to because children can inadvertently find pornography so easily. Once your children reach the pre-teenage years I would also combine accountability software. It is just as important to know what your 14-year-old son *tried to* look at, as it is to know what he actually managed to look at. I'm not a big fan of porn blockers for adults, unless it is used in combination with accountability software. It is too easy for a porn blocker to become a game where you search to see if there are any sites that you get through to. There is a gambling-sort of thrill you get when you finally "score" and beat the system.Still, there are sites that I don't even want to allow myself to be able to view and there is material that is too egregious to see even momentarily. I use OpenDNS as my Domain Name Service[3], which has multiple filtering options, in concert with accountability software (Covenant Eyes) as a safeguard of either inadvertent or intentional access to material that is way off the charts.

---

3. http://opendns.org is a free service that replaces your existing domain name service (the thing that turns site names into IP addresses) with what usually results in a faster lookup, and has over 40 levels of domain-based filtering. Read more about it at their web site..

For Accountability Partners

What if you're an accountability partner for some-body else? Are there any special guidelines for that job description?

An accountability relationship, porn blockers, and accountability software are necessary, however, they will be insufficient to produce real change. True spiritual growth in the Lord is the ultimate solution. As we dis-cussed in the last chapter, Romans 12 says the only way to not be "conformed to this world" is to be "transformed by the renewing of your mind." This transformation is the goal, not just a cessation of sin. The grace and love of God is fundamental here. Be sure to hold out for a high view of that. Make sure you both understand that moralistic solutions or a focus on managing behaviors will quickly become just another form of idolatry and will fail to produce the fruit of righteousness that God promises us.

Having said that, in order to help your friend, it is useful to understand something of the pathology of sexual sin. You also need to know more about the person you are helping. Consider having them write up a sexual sin "history" where they describe how they got into sexual sin, how long it has been going on, and the kinds of sexual material and activities they have been in to. Encourage them to "go deep," to not leave things out, but to avoid sordid details. These memories can be painful, and also trigger sinful episodes, so make it clear you are not look-ing for a pornographic autobiography, but a full frank disclosure.

Go over this paper with your friend, but do not keep

it. It's their history, and you would not want to have
something in your possession that could be used against
them. It might not even be a bad idea to burn it with them
after you've gone over it together. Also, consider asking
about co-addictions in the person's life – alcohol, gam-
bling, excessive television and video games and so forth.
These can be further expressions of the same spiritual
and personal emptiness that is behind their addiction
to porn. Get regular time together. Just asking how it's
going when you're standing in a group of people after a
church meeting can't possibly foster the kind of openness that is required. You should have a good portion of
time alone together so you can go over how things have
been going recently, and pray together. Frequent time
together will help you keep short accounts, and not allow
sin and guilt to move the person away from the Lord. The
frequency of your time together should be determined
by how new that person's commitment is, but I would
suggest weekly at first.

The question of confidentiality is a tough one to
answer in black and white, but you need to be certain
that the person feels safe talking to you. Not everything
your friend does needs to be talked about with others,
though there certainly may be times where they should
be encouraged to share with others. It's not your job
to confess for them. In the long run, they should be
able to widen the circle of accountability, but it's not a
requirement, especially in the earlier stages of this kind
of relationship.

Check up on *provisional* aspects of recovery—those
things we do as a matter of course to build our spiritual

lives. There should be regular time spent in the Word, prayer, and other means of spiritual growth. There should be steps taken to build relationships and minister to the needs of others, which provide a framework for intimacy and accomplishment. These are just as important as whether or not a person has had a recent episode of sexual sin.

Check up on *momentary* aspects of recovery—those things we do before, during, and after times of temptation. It's important to know what was going on in the person's life and thinking just prior to a period of temptation. What was the person thinking about? Did they judge their thoughts? Did they count the cost? Did they think about the benefits of their relationship with God? These kinds of questions will remind your friend of the value of living an examined life. We are free in His grace and we have the mind of Christ; we are not animals controlled by our impulses. Encourage them to think about their actions when they are tempted. After a failure in this area, ask them how they thought about God and themselves. Use this time to remind them of the grace of God, and His complete accessibility.

We have a real enemy who is powerful, and has built a system that surrounds us at all times to move us from the purity of following Christ. Has the person you're helping been praying against the devil? Encourage them to engage in regular spiritual warfare (see the next chapter).

Sexual sin is a false intimacy. One of the steps that they need to take is to move toward genuine intimacy with others, and to be involved in other people's lives. Has your friend been moving toward others, or back towards isolation? If married, are they moving toward their spouse relationally and sexually? Are there other barriers to relationship that need to be explored?

It would not be practical to talk about all the items on the above list every time you get together. You should vary your discussion to address different aspects of spiritual growth and not always dwell on how they're dealing with temptation. Sexual sin is usually a secondary issue to other things in a person's life. If your time together is always focused on managing your friend's sin life, you won't provide the level of help that is needed.

If you're an accountability partner for another person, this is an important role that you're playing. As you work together, God will honor your efforts to bring Christ more into focus as the true provider of "everything that we need for life and godliness." My hope is that this role will be enriching for both of you.

For Group Discussion

Share what's been going on with you lately. Rejoice in any victories someone has had, and encourage those who have not been doing as well.

Talk about your own history of hiding, lack of honesty with others, presenting a false persona to others. What was the outcome? How might you have handled things differently? What do you think the outcome would have been?

Which (expert or spectator) do you tend to be? How are your tendencies influencing your relationships?

How have you practiced accountability partnering in the past? What were some successes and failures? How can you incorporate what you learned from this chapter to make accountability partnering be a helpful tool in the battle against sexual sin and pornography?

Pray for each member in your group. Ask God to give you opportunities for a meaningful accountability relationship with another, thanking him that by the power of grace we can be set free from deception in our relationships.

EIGHT

THE BATTLE

The following testimony comes from one of the ladies in our ministry who has struggled with pornography since childhood, and learned how to deal with the onslaught of temptation by the Devil through the word of God and prayer. Though the other testimonies in this book come from men, it's important to see how this is not just a male problem; She has graciously shared her story with us.

"I was first exposed to pornography when I was 11 years old. I had been struggling against my pornography addiction for 10 years when I finally confessed to a fellow sister in Christ. Those 10 years I kept trying to stop cold turkey, telling myself "this is the last time," but I eventually was back in sin again. I kept trying to fight temptation out of my own strength, but I also didn't know anything about spiritual warfare, that it was real and I was in the thick of it.

Spiritual warfare has always been difficult for to me understand because it seems so abstract. However, actively fighting against attack gave me a new perspective and fighting was no easy task. My heart would ache and my soul was writhing in the pain of feeling lonely, worthless and hopeless.

The real battle began when I realized that I was making a choice. I was not helpless; I was actively choosing to sin. A verse that helped me to understand the importance of this choice was Romans 12:1. I began to understand that how I handled my body could actually be an act of worship for God. Instead of choosing to sin, I would choose to worship God by presenting my body, my aches, my pains, and my choice as a sacrifice. I committed other verses to memory, which proved to be helpful in prayer as I called on God for help. When I started to feel lonely or worthless I would pray, often with tears, asking for His strength. I confessed that I didn't have the power to fight and that I desperately needed Him. Often, by the time I was done praying, the temptation was gone and I could easily drift off to sleep.

After having victory over my sin for a solid 3 months, I got hit with an intense dream that I had given into my temptation again. My friends were disgusted with me and I felt ashamed. I woke up frightened and shaking, feeling gross, guilty, and alienated. I immediately told my roommate and we prayed together. Soon afterwards, I felt a weight had been lifted. I had a few more vivid dreams after that, and sometimes I still have them. But I know how to fight against attack and that's been a great comfort for me.

To put it simply, prayer paired with scripture is powerful. It gave me victory in battle and rescued me from myself."

You and I are caught up in the greatest war that has ever been fought. It started before time when Satan rebelled against God and rejected his authority. It will culminate at the end of history when Satan will be vanquished and thrown into the "lake of fire" having had his power to deceive hearts utterly destroyed (Revelations 20:10).

The war that is being fought is about truth and especially about truth as it relates to God. It is a battle of ideas where lies and deception are Satan's primary tools against mankind. So it was in the Garden of Eden— "did God really say?" and "you surely shall not die"—when Satan twisted the truth while he talked to Eve. So too, he used the same strategy when he tempted Jesus in the desert— "If you, then, will worship me, it [all the kingdoms of the world] will all be yours." Satan is a liar, the very father of lies (John 8:44), and his goal is to deceive men so that they will join him in throwing off God's authority.

In the life of the Christian the battle is for our hearts, our affections, our inclinations, and our passions. Satan can create nothing; he can only use what God has given us in his efforts to draw our hearts away from the Creator. It doesn't matter to Satan *where* our hearts are drawn, as long as they are captured by something other than God himself. To achieve his goals, Satan will use lies about God ("he could never love me") and ourselves ("I need this pleasure right now") while he leverages both our doubts and the latent selfish power of our sin nature.

For those of us who battle against the temptation of sexual sin, Satan will take every advantage to draw us into moral failure. He'll work in clever ways to deceive us, actively tempt us, and take advantage of our self-centered sin nature in order to accomplish his goal. Yet, I don't think that sexual sin in itself is his ultimate goal. He doesn't really care how we are drawn away, only that we are. Besides tempting us to sin, he has additional goals in mind:

- the perversion of God's gift of sex
- drawing our hearts away from God into the world system
- extinguishing our dream of living for the glory of God

The Perversion of God's Gift of Sex

In his fictional depiction of demonic temptation, *The Screwtape Letters*, C.S. Lewis gives us an interesting insight when his protagonist says:

"Never forget that when we are dealing with any pleasure in its healthy and normal and satisfying form, we are, in a sense, on the Enemy's [God's] ground. I know we have won many a soul through pleasure. All the same, it is His invention, not ours. He made the pleasures: all our research so far has not enabled us to produce one. All we can do is to encourage the humans to take the pleasures which our Enemy has produced, at times, or in ways, or in degrees which He has forbidden. Hence we always try to work away from the natural condition of any pleasure to that in which it is least natural, least redolent of its Maker, and least pleasurable. An ever-increasing craving for an ever diminishing pleasure is the formula."[1]

Sex was meant to increase intimacy between people by reinforcing it with pleasure. Satan wants to convince us of the following lies:

- Sex is about *pleasure*, not intimacy - If pleasure is your only goal, you will miss out on the unique joys of intimacy with another person. If Satan can remove the real joy of spiritual intimacy in sex, he can leave us with only emptiness.

- Sex is about *taking* what you want, not giving - Seeing sex as simply taking what we want from another person demeans them as merely an extension of our selfishness.

- Sex is about the *physical* only, not the spiritual - When sexual satisfaction is oriented only around physical pleasure we will get only enough of a taste of that fulfillment to be left hungry. Deceived and driven to find satisfaction, we crave more sex, different sex, sex with more partners, more explicit pornography, or more frequent masturbation. We find ourselves unsatisfied and empty. Satan has tempted us down a path that ends only in more desire, never deep joy or satisfaction.

Our enemy would have us pursue pleasure but never truly find it. The Bible asserts that the greatest pleasure is to know and love God, and to love others sacrificially. When sex is pursued in a committed relationship in the

---

1. C.S. Lewis, *The Screwtape Letters*, (Harper Collins, New York, 1996), 52

context of that greater love it is profoundly satisfying. We have the privilege of knowing and enjoying our partner uniquely while we also honor the Author and Creator of pleasure.

The Message of the World System

The New Testament uses the term *kosmos* to describe the world system. It is Satan's kingdom and it is hostile towards God. In his first epistle, John describes the basic ideology of the *kosmos*:

> "Do not love the world nor the things in the world. If anyone loves the world, the love of the Father is not in him. For all that is in the world, the lust of the flesh and the lust of the eyes and the boastful pride of life, is not from the Father, but is from the world. The world is passing away, and also its lusts; but the one who does the will of God lives forever. (1 John 2:15–17, NASB)

The three "lusts" or "cravings"—the lust of the flesh, the lust of the eyes, and the boastful pride of life—converge in the world of pornography. The physical craving for orgasm is elevated as the most important event in life. The objectification of the human body (even the individual parts of the body) airbrushed to idealized perfection is offered up to our lusting eyes.

The boastful pride of man is extolled in pornography. He takes what he wants in a virtual world where he has ultimate power over the bodies of women (whether they like it or not) even to the point of virtual rape.

Pornography perfectly reflects the orientation of "the god of this world, who has blinded the eyes of the unbelieving." (2 Corinthians 4:4) It's hard to think of anything more in tune with the spirit of our age than man, isolated and alone, clicking slavishly away as image after image passes before his eyes to feed his lust — a virtual Vanity Fair of idolatry and hopelessness.

John tells us that this world, this *kosmos*, is passing away, along with its lusts. The world that will replace it will be marked by joy that will so far surpass the lusts of this world that we can scarcely imagine the difference. Perhaps C.S. Lewis comes close in his sermon, The Weight of Glory, where he says, "We are half-hearted creatures, fooling about with drink and sex and ambition when infinite joy is offered us, like an ignorant child who wants to go on making mud pies in a slum because he cannot imagine what is meant by the offer of a holiday at the sea. We are far too easily pleased."[2]

The Extinguisher of Dreams

Have you ever had a dream of serving God with your whole life? Have you had a big-thinking, radical passionate dream of being fully committed to God and his work and a life of fruitfulness? When I first became a Christian in 1974 I was immediately consumed with the vision of what God could do through my so-far wasted life. I had been redeemed and given a chance to live for something other than the approval of men and selfish pleasure. I was going to be among those who turned the world upside-down.

That sort of dream was not just a product of naïve

---

2. Lewis, C. S., & Dorsett, L. W.. *The essential C.S. Lewis.* (Simon and Schuster, 1996), 362

youthfulness (I was in college at the time); God planted that dream in my heart. We are all meant to live for Christ. We have the opportunity to become thoroughly engaged in what God is doing in human history and to have our hearts caught up in his plan to bring the gospel to all nations and peoples. "And he died for all, that those who live might no longer live for themselves but for him who for their sake died and was raised" (2 Corinthians 5:15).

As I began to struggle with the failure of sexual sin later in my Christian life, the song of the dream that God had put in my heart began to grow faint, and I began to hear another song, that of the world system. There were disappointments in my ministry and moral failure in my home. It seemed that I was never going to experience the future I had envisioned. Satan was using my failures to get me to forget my dream. I was ashamed because I wasn't following God's will for my sexuality and I began to look for something to fulfill me so that I could forget how bad I felt inside.

Of course, the *kosmos* offers money, power in the workplace, fancy clothes, and golf courses. Those never really satisfied me though. Even as I kept thinking that it might somehow be possible to align my life with God's plan, lust and self-seeking pleasure anesthetized my brain. At one point I figured that any possible effectiveness for God had come to an end and I could forget the dream. I could be an ordinary man, living a life of quiet, if comfortable, desperation.

Then, God showed me something amazing in Paul's first letter to Timothy:

"I thank him who has given me strength, Christ Jesus our Lord, because he judged me faithful, appointing me to his service, though formerly I was a blasphemer, persecutor, and insolent opponent. But I received mercy because I had acted ignorantly in unbelief, and the grace of our Lord overflowed for me with the faith and love that are in Christ Jesus. The saying is trustworthy and deserving of full acceptance, that Christ Jesus came into the world to save sinners, of whom I am the foremost. But I received mercy for this reason, that in me, as the foremost, Jesus Christ might display his perfect patience as an example to those who were to believe in him for eternal life." (1 Tim. 1:12-16)

I realized as I read that passage that Paul's calling did not come from his personal righteousness, but rather directly from the fact that he had received mercy. Paul could have spent his Christian life feeling bad about having been a blasphemer and persecutor of the church and been defined by the memory of those sins. Instead, he saw how his qualification for ministry came from the mercy of God for those sins. It hit me like a ton of bricks. My former sins were not what were holding me back; it was the lies of the enemy that had quenched the flame. I could still live that dream because God saw me clothed with Christ's righteousness and had called me into faithful service.

Satan wants more than anything to keep you defeated over your past sins. He cannot rob you of the forgiveness you have in Christ, but he can steal away your joy, your commitment to your Lord, your passion for his glory, demonstrated through a life of obedience and service. A defeated Christian, weighed down with guilt over past disobedience, gladdens Satan's heart. Are you going to let him do that to you?

Spiritual Warfare – Your Role in the Battle

As long as our enemy has you enslaved to lust, he need do little else; he holds the day. When you decide to move towards God he will move in with temptation and accusation. You must stand your ground. You must strive in faith to believe God and work against him in your thought life, in prayer, and in taking action.

In Thought

We must work against the devil in our thought life because Satan is the great deceiver. Jesus said Satan "always hated the truth. There is no truth in him. When he lies, it is consistent with his character; for he is a liar and the father of lies" (John 8:44). Deceit may be his strongest weapon against you, because of how using pornography distorts your thinking. We've already looked at 2 Corinthians 10:5 in terms of our thought life, but we need to think about its context as well – spiritual warfare.

> "For though we walk in the flesh, we do not war according to the flesh, for the weapons of our warfare are not of the flesh, but divinely powerful for the destruction of fortresses. We are destroying speculations and every lofty thing raised up against the knowledge of God, and we are taking every thought captive to the obedience of Christ" (2 Corinthians 10:3-5).

Never forget who your real enemy is: it is not pornography, or the people who produce it, or the unscrupulous people who put near-naked women on your favorite news feed to draw your attention. Our enemy is a spiritual being, bent on drawing our hearts away from God, but we are armed with spiritual weapons to fight this battle. It's a battle of ideas: what is life about, what's important, what do I need most? It's a battle against the ideological strongholds—or fortresses—that have been erected against the truth in my mind. These ideas are alive in our culture, but also in our hearts and thinking.

The defining characteristic of our thought life in the midst of this battle is *alertness*. "...for you are all sons of light and sons of day. We are not of night nor of darkness; so then let us not sleep as others do, but let us be alert and sober" (1 Thessalonians 5:5-6). "Be self-controlled and alert. Your enemy the devil prowls around like a roaring lion looking for someone to devour" (1 Peter 5:8).

Practically speaking, alertness is the action of actively watching over your own life. It means that you know where temptation might be strongest and what sorts of things trigger you to turn to sex for fulfillment. There are situations that you know you should avoid. Alertness means that you actually choose to avoid them. For example, my wife often teaches all-day classes on Saturdays. As an empty nester I could sleep in late, do things around the house, or study on the back porch in solitary bliss, but I don't. I hit the gym early, hang out with brothers, and study at a coffee shop until she's off work. Why? Because I know myself, and being alone in the house all day long is a temptation to me. Alertness means that I avoid those kinds of temptations. Other men can stay at home alone all day — not me.

Alertness also means knowing how you will deal with stress. A serious setback in a relationship, or difficulties at work or school can put a lot of stress on you. Alertness means that I know that I have a history of handling stress with sinful entitlement. When I encounter stress I remind myself, "You know that you have a tendency to handle stress with sin. It's time to get before the Lord, or talk to another brother about what's going on."

We practice alertness not by just seeing the strongholds, but by destroying them in the power of God's word. The good news of the gospel is that we are very well armed "by truthful speech, and the power of God; with the weapons of righteousness for the right hand and for the left" (2 Corinthians 6:7). Taking our thoughts captive to the obedience of Christ means vigorously challenging these ideas with the truth: reading it, meditating on it, praying it, singing it, letting the light of the glory of the gospel sink into your heart.

While practicing this kind of alertness is the first line of defense against our enemy, we need to do battle in prayer as well.

In Prayer

> "Finally, be strong in the Lord and in his mighty power. Put on the full armor of God so that you can take your stand against the devil's schemes... And pray in the Spirit on all occasions with all kinds of prayers and requests. With this in mind, be alert and always keep on praying for all the saints." (Ephesians 6:10-18)

Our strength is in the Lord, not in ourselves. We have no intrinsic power against the forces of spiritual darkness. The power that raised Jesus Christ from the dead is the only power that we have, and it's all that we will ever need. This is a defensive battle ("take your stand"), and the devil wants to take the ground that God has claimed in your life. As you trust Him and rely on His strength, you show Satan that you mean to keep what you have earned, and advance further. Paul calls for "all kinds of prayer" – praying for alertness, praying against temptation, praying for growth, praying to know Christ more and more, praying for Him to be your greatest love, and praying for others.

Praying against the devil in your life is crucial. It's how you align yourself with the power of God to hold the ground you've taken and take even new ground against the forces of evil. Chuck Smith of Calvary Chapel in Costa Mesa has a great book on prayer called *Effective Prayer Life*. In it, he has a section on waging war with the devil in prayer, called *The Battle*. He writes:

> "Satan is a very stubborn enemy and an obstinate fighter. He yields only what and when he must. Therefore, your prayers must be very specific. Vague, general prayers like "God, save the world" won't even dent the enemy. But when you bring before the Lord an individual life and lay claim to that person for Jesus Christ, you begin to be specific in prayer, Satan must yield."[3]

3. Smith, Chuck. *Effective Prayer Life*. (The Word for Today, 1980), 11

Have you specifically prayed about your problem with lust? Have you asked the Lord to free you? Have you also prayed against the enemy of your progress? Have you prayed specifically, in detail, about very specific situations and temptations that Satan tempts you in, or accuses you for? Have you prayed against your favorite fantasies and fetishes? Have you prayed that God would help you see the lies of Satan for what they are? To do so is to claim the ground of victory that Jesus purchased for you at the cross.

Many of you have experienced the accusation of the devil. You have been tempted into sinning, and while your conscience is aroused in protest, the accuser steps in to tell you what a terrible person you are, how God could never love or use you in his service. This sort of accusation can be grievous to our souls, and has convinced many Christians that they might as well give up the fight. They wonder: what is the use? Why bother trying to follow God; I'm only going to fail again! The focus of this accusation is always on the old self. If we belong to God, we must remember that our old self died at the cross with Christ.

Satan's lies about us seem true only if we ignore what God says about who we are in Christ. "For I am the least of the apostles, unworthy to be called an apostle, because I persecuted the church of God. But by the grace of God I am what I am, and his grace toward me was not in vain" (1 Corinthians 15:9-10).

Who you are is what you are by the grace of God! Your old identity doesn't matter any longer, because you have a new nature, a new identity, and a new role in life.

This is not God's witness protection program, it's a life made new!

> "What am I? I am forgiven, I am reconciled to God by the Blood of His Son upon the Cross. I am a child of God. I am adopted into God's family, and I am an heir with Christ, a joint-heir with Him. I am going to glory. That is what matters, not what I was, not what I have been."[4]

Our identity in Christ is what counts, and we need to remember in our prayers what God says is true of us. Give thanks to him for the person he has made you: a royal son, beloved and cherished, protected from the assaults of the evil one. Praise him for the salvation that he has brought you freely and the assurance that he will keep you until the end. Tell the devil in your prayers (and I believe he is listening) about the ground you stand upon, bought for you by Christ who vanquished him.

Martin Luther is claimed to have said the following:

> "When I go to bed, the devil is always waiting for me. When he begins to plague me, I give him this answer: 'Devil, I must sleep. That's God's command — work by day, sleep by night. So go away.' If that doesn't work and he brings out a catalog of sins, I say, 'Yes, old fellow, I know all about it. And I know some more you have overlooked. Here are a few extra. Put them down.' If he still won't quit and presses me hard and accuses me as a sinner, I scorn him and say, 'St. Satan, pray for me. Of

4. Lloyd-Jones, D. M. *Spiritual depression: its causes and cure*. (Wm. B. Eerdmans Publishing, 1980), 86

course, you have never done anything wrong in your life. You alone are holy. Go to God and get grace for yourself. If you want to get me all straightened out, I say, Physician, heal thyself.'"[5]

That's confidence in grace! Claim the power of the cross and you can be bold even in the face of temptation and accusation.

In Action

"Be self-controlled and alert. Your enemy the devil prowls around like a roaring lion looking for someone to devour. Resist him, standing firm in the faith, because you know that your brothers throughout the world are undergoing the same kind of sufferings. And the God of all grace, who called you to his eternal glory in Christ, after you have suffered a little while, will himself restore you and make you strong, firm and steadfast." (1 Peter 5:8-10)

We must resist the devil. What does that really look like? Paul puts it this way: "The night is almost gone, and the day is near. Therefore let us lay aside the deeds of darkness and put on the armor of light" (Romans 13:12). "Now flee from youthful lusts and pursue righteousness, faith, love and peace, with those who call on the Lord from a pure heart" (2 Timothy 2:22). Take a look at the contrasting verbs here – "lay aside… and put on," "flee… and pursue." We must always be putting on the armor of our salvation and pursuing righteousness, faith, love,

5. Bainton, R., *Here I Stand - A Life of Martin Luther*, (Read Books, 2007), 362

and peace. This is faith in action, not just mental assent. It's standing firm in our faith, holding on to the power of the gospel.

Faith in action means orienting our life around the things of the Spirit. It's building loving relationships. It's taking your identity as one who is in Christ, who has been delivered from the domain of darkness and transferred to the kingdom of the Son. Resistance in action is living the Christian life. No matter what you may have done, you move toward God, the source of life and light. It is resistance in action when we refuse to adopt our enemy's perspective in the areas of worldliness and living for sensuality, comfort, and pride and when we instead make our lives about investing in the people Christ died to redeem.

When we do that, the enemy of God will flee from us.

For Group Discussion:

Talk about how things have been going for you since you last met. Confess any sins and share any victories over temptation.

How has the mentality of the world system and our mutual enemy affected your views of sex?

In what ways has your experience trying to follow God's plan for your sexuality been like a battle?

What steps can you take in the battle? What does resistance look like for you? Be specific about actions you can start taking immediately.

Pray for each member in your group. Ask God to open your eyes to the spiritual battle going on around you, and in your own heart. Thank him for his power over darkness, and the victory he gained at the cross.

NINE

TEMPTATION AND FAILURE

L ife is full of temptations. The world, the flesh, and the devil conspire against us. We are enticed to seek happiness, fulfillment, and pleasure in ways that dishonor God. These things become ends in themselves and will enslave us instead of satisfying us.

We are not self-sufficient and self-directed. In truth we are by nature merely responders. We are dependent worshippers. God designed us to be mastered by his loving leadership, but in chasing after other things we delude ourselves into thinking we are our own masters. Often, it is too late once we realize that something or someone else is mastering us.

Temptation is where that all begins. Once we belong to Christ, our sin nature is rendered powerless in itself to dominate us. However, that nature continues to wait with bated breath for its opportunity to regain control. Satan and his kingdom have a surplus of schemes for the flesh to take center stage. Whether it's porn, joining in on gossip, or another piece of chocolate cake, temptation is an invitation to choose. Every day we are presented with a myriad of choices. The way we navigate through them determines the course that our life takes and the kind of person we become.

The World

The preponderance of sexual images in our modern culture is unprecedented. A simple visit to a nearby mall can feel more like a visual assault than a shopping trip. There is no form of media that is not full of suggestive images. Sex is used to sell everything from clothes to cars to soap. I probably don't need to say anything more about it, because you already know this. Our culture has gone from repressed to obsessed in a very short time.

The fashion industry is making sure that the message is clear that skin is in. Unlike the fig leaves that formed the first clothing, it seems that the point of the fashion industry is to uncover nakedness. Are thongs really comfortable? What is the point of low-rise "skinny jeans" and cropped shirts? Whatever the intent of the fashion designer, the effect on men is simple: temptation.

The Internet has an unprecedented aggregation of suggestive material. Along with the close to five million pornography web sites, there are banner ads everywhere that use pictures of scantily-clad girls to entice you to look at advertisements. From Facebook to Fox News these smiling sirens of sensuality beckon you into a world of lust.

The Flesh

The world around us assaults our senses, attempting to lure us away from the Lord. Even without that though, temptation is as close as you are. You can avoid the mall and the magazine rack, cancel your cable TV subscription, and stomp your laptop into pieces, but what has been seen can never be unseen. So the videos in your mind, whether those things you have seen or imagined, can continue to parade before you. This too can lead you into temptation. The flesh is persistent and asserts itself at every opportunity. For example, you may have quit looking at pornography, but notice that you start having sexual dreams more frequently, or still find yourself being consumed with lustful thoughts during the day. This is a common experience for men in recovery, and it is a sign that the flesh is trying to reassert its dominion.

Our flesh, the sin nature, demands to be fed with those things that make it stronger. It works tirelessly to oppose the work that God is doing in our lives:

> "For I know that nothing good dwells in me, that is, in my flesh. . .I myself serve the law of God with my mind, but with my flesh I serve the law of sin." (Romans 7:18, 25)

> "For the mind that is set on the flesh is hostile to God, for it does not submit to God's law; indeed, it cannot." (Romans 8:7)

> "For the desires of the flesh are against the Spirit, and the desires of the Spirit are against the flesh, for these are opposed to each other, to keep you from doing the things you want to do." (Galatians 5:17)

> "Beloved, I urge you as sojourners and exiles to abstain from the passions of the flesh, which wage war against your soul." (1 Peter 2:11)

Your old sin nature will always try to convince you that the rewards of giving in are more sweet than the rewards of obedience. If you were alone on a desert island, you would still be tempted to lust, pride, anger, envy, deceit, and malice. Removing yourself from the world and its temptations is no way to escape. I believe that this can be one of the problems with some programs aimed at helping people escape the grip of pornography: they focus on removing the pornography before our eyes, but leave the porn behind our eyes to plague us with none to vanquish its power.

The Devil

In the last chapter we talked about the devil's tactics against us. The temptations of God's enemy are clever and insidious. They often come at us mostly from the world system that he presides over. Satan and his minions may also tempt us directly. Though I'm not certain that Satan can read your mind, he is brilliant, and an acute student of human behavior. He probably knows your "buttons" better than you do. Like a skilled fisherman who understands exactly which fly to tie for a particular fish, stream, and type of weather, so too Satan know precisely what will seduce you.

The genius of Satan's tactics against followers of Christ is the one-two punch of temptation and accusation. His leadoff pitch of "Come on, go and ahead and do it – it's no big deal" is always followed by moral outrage "How could you, a Christian, do something like that?" We must be prepared for this tactic, "so that we would not be outwitted by Satan; for we are not ignorant of his designs." (2 Corinthians 2:11) Remember that the primary tactic of Satan in temptation is to move us away from God and his grace.

How Do We Deal with Temptation?

> "No temptation has seized you except what is
> common to man. And God is faithful; he will not
> let you be tempted beyond what you can bear. But
> when you are tempted, he will also provide a way
> out so that you can stand up under it."
> (1 Corinthians 10:13)

We learn several things from this verse. First, what you
are going through is not something unusual. As Chuck
Palahniuk says in *Fight Club*: "you are not a beautiful and
unique snowflake."[1] We all think that our temptation is
singular, unique, that no one else has ever faced what we
are facing. Our first assurance from 1 Corinthians 10:13
is that what you are going through is a shared experience.
There are others who understand your struggles with
whom you can band together. "So flee youthful passions
and pursue righteousness, faith, love, and peace, along
with those who call on the Lord from a pure heart" (2
Timothy 2:22). When we confess our sins in fellowship
with others, we find out that they are dealing with the
same temptations. That's one reason why it's so important
to band together with other brothers.

The Faithfulness of God

Next, Paul reminds us of the faithfulness of God.
These simple words, "God is faithful" are so very powerful. How faithful is God?

> I will never leave you or forsake you. (Hebrews
> 13:5)

---

1. Palahniuk, Chuck, *Fight Club*, (W.W. Norton & Co, 1996),134

"I am with you always, even to the end of the age."
(Matthew 28:20)

"If we are faithless, He remains faithful for He
cannot deny Himself." (2 Timothy 2:13)

"Since he did not spare even his own Son but gave
him up for us all, won't he also give us everything
else?" (Romans 8:32, NLT)

"But the Lord is faithful. He will establish you and
guard you against the evil one."
(2 Thessalonians 3:3)

God is the one person in the universe who is totally
faithful, who always does exactly what He says he will do.
Go back and read those words, because they are intended
for you. If you belong to Him, God is faithful to you at
all times because He cannot deny Himself.

No Temptation Too Great?

Everybody has a breaking point, a temptation that
is too great. I'm certain that there are situations I could
get into where I would fall. This verse promises that
no matter how great the temptation, the power of God
in your favor will always be greater. I have seen this in
action many times. Earlier, when I was deeply involved
with pornography, I had several opportunities to take
things to the next level, with more "personal" involve-
ments in sexual sin. However, God always delivered me
from those possibilities. I believe with all my heart that
he was protecting me from going down a path that I
would not return from without deep damage to my soul

and marriage.

I used to attend Sexaholics Anonymous and Sex Addict Anonymous 12-step meetings. As I sat and listened to the stories of the men there, at first I was glad I had never done any of the things I was hearing. There were men who had engaged in sex with hundreds of anonymous partners, men who had spent the mortgage money on strip clubs and massage parlors, men who had sexually imposed themselves on children. It was pretty rough. After a while, though, I realized that I was only about three decisions away from becoming any one of them. What had held me back? I could only conclude that the Spirit of God living within me had been protecting my heart, and my sovereign Father was guiding my path away from evil opportunities.

This verse does not promise that God will always prevent you from getting in to sin. He won't always have your wife or roommate walk in just as you're about to open the browser. What he will always do is provide a way that you can escape. You will never be so tempted that there is no way out for you. You are no longer enslaved to sin (Romans 6). You always have a choice to turn to God, who freely accepts you because of Christ's work on the cross on your behalf.

What Is the Way of Escape?

When you are trying to escape temptation, I don't think the form of your escape is as important as the pace. Once a lustful thought implants itself in your brain, you don't have much time. In Genesis 39, when Potiphar's wife tried to seduce him, Joseph fled so quickly that he left his outer garment behind. Paul tells Timothy to "flee youthful lusts." If you allow lust to captivate you and give it time to entangle you in its clutches, you are far more likely to fall into the trap. Don't give the flesh an opportunity when you know you are tempted; get moving quickly!

John Piper recommends an approach (with the acronym ANTHEM) that addresses this:[2]

A – AVOID, as much as is possible and reasonable, the sights and situations that arouse unfitting desire.

N – Say NO to every lustful thought within five seconds.

T – TURN the mind forcefully toward Christ as a superior satisfaction.

H – HOLD the promise and the pleasure of Christ firmly in your mind until it pushes the other images out.

E – ENJOY a superior satisfaction.

M – MOVE into a useful activity away from idleness and other vulnerable behaviors.

Talking to Yourself

D. Martyn Lloyd-Jones said, "We must talk to ourselves, instead of allowing ourselves to talk to us."[3] This is sound advice for us when we face temptation. Our sin nature is always talking to us, jabbering away about how

---

2. See http://www.desiringgod.org/resource-library/ taste-see-articles/anthem-strategies-for-fighting-lust

3. Lloyd-Jones, D. M., *Spiritual depression: its causes and cure*, (Wm. B. Eerdmans Publishing, 1965)

exciting it will be, how much we deserve a break, how it won't cause any harm. It's time to talk back.

We must talk to ourselves in two ways: negatively and positively. What if I told you there was a device that you could purchase that, when you pressed a button, would give you a 5-minute rush of instant pleasure and well being, something like crystal meth meets heroin? It would have no long-term side effects and last for 100 uses. You might be intrigued by a device like that! What if I told you that it costs $50,000? You would immediately say: that's not worth it!

What if I told you that continually subjecting yourself that sexual sin is just as costly, more so even? This is exactly what the Bible teaches: sin leads to bondage, shame, and death – a heavy cost!

> "Don't you know that when you offer yourselves to someone to obey him as slaves, you are slaves to the one whom you obey—whether you are slaves to sin, which leads to death, or to obedience, which leads to righteousness? …What benefit did you reap at that time from the things you are now ashamed of? Those things result in death! "
> (Romans 6:16, 21 NIV)

Have you thought about indulging in sin as throwing yourself into bondage, slavery, and death? That's how you should be thinking about it in those moments of temptation. Count the cost. It will cost you your present fellowship with God. It will also compromise your ability to relate deeply to your wife or friends. Will it affect your sleep or your wallet? Will you feel shame in the morning? Will you feel embarrassed when you confess it to someone or when they see your accountability report? Is it worth the loss of your spiritual effectiveness, your job, your marriage, even your kids? The Bible is clear that living for sin will cost you your life.

When you think about it that way, maybe you will decide that the porn moment isn't worth it. Many times this is an effective strategy against temptation in the moment. However, over the long haul, negative consequences alone are not sufficiently powerful against the lure of sin. You will need much more than negative reinforcement.

Consider what can be gained when you flee from temptation: the sweetness of experiencing the love of God. Be compelled by the joy of having fellowship with Him, your wife, your brothers, your kids. Be inspired by the satisfaction that comes from obedience to Christ, and the joy of serving him. As we learn to love Jesus and rejoice in what He has done for us, our obedience changes from wanting to avoid the negative consequences to wanting to experience fellowship with Him.

> "But now that you have been set free from sin and
> have become slaves of God, the fruit you get leads
> to sanctification and its end, eternal life."
> (Romans 6:22)

Now ask yourself: do I want to trade those benefits for the fleeting pleasure of sin? Have you ever read the story of Esau? Esau, the firstborn son of a prosperous father, sold his birthright to his brother Jacob in exchange for some lentil soup. No matter how tasty that soup was, it wasn't worth it, and Esau wept bitterly when he realized what he had done (Genesis 25, 27). The writer of

Hebrews warns us,

> "See to it that no one fails to obtain the grace of God; that no "root of bitterness" springs up and causes trouble, and by it many become defiled; that no one is sexually immoral or unholy like Esau, who sold his birthright for a single meal."
> (Hebrews 12:15–16)

Like Esau, we can sell our peace with God for an orgasm. As you begin to truly value your walk with God, that will seem more and more like the bad deal it is. The trick is to make that analysis during the point of temptation, not after.

Faith and Unbelief

The choices you make during temptation find their root in faith or unbelief. The point of attack isn't just against our desires, but against what we believe to be true. Whenever we live like the pleasures of sin are better than the pleasures of God, we are in unbelief. We have forgotten the cross and our redemption; we have forgotten that we are new creatures, formed in the image of Christ; we have forgotten that we have a new calling, to live lives that find their greatest fulfillment in others, and not ourselves. C.S. Lewis puts it this way:

> "I think one may be quite rid of the old haunting suspicion — which raises its head in every temptation — that there is something else than God, some other country into which he forbids us to trespass, some kind of delight which he 'doesn't appreciate' or just chooses to forbid, but which would be real delight if only we were allowed to get it. The

thing *just isn't there*. Whatever we desire is either
what God is trying to give us as quickly as he can,
or else a false picture of what he is trying to give
us, a false picture which would not attract us for a
moment if we saw the real thing… He knows what
we want, even in our vilest acts. He is longing to
give it to us… The truth is that evil is not a real
thing at all, like God. It is simply good spoiled…
You know what the biologists mean by a parasite
— an animal that lives on another animal. Evil is a
parasite. It is there only because good is there for
it to spoil and confuse."[4]

John Piper also talks about the relationship between
our sin and unbelief:

"Unbelief relates like this: my understanding of
faith is that you don't just believe that Jesus as the
Son of God died for your sins, rose again, reigns
in heaven, is coming again, and forgives my sin.
That's only factual. It's also being satisfied with
that, treasuring that. Faith is not just an intellectual
assent to doctrines. Faith is an affectional embrace
of the Savior for my deepest longings.

Unbelief, on the other hand, is a failure to be satisfied in Jesus. It's a failure to go to him as the
Living Water and the Bread from heaven and the
Light of the world. It's a failure to go to him as a
satisfaction that's deep enough and strong enough
to satisfy me when I am tempted to go in a sinful

4. C.S. Lewis, cited in Walter Hooper, editor, *They Stand Together*
(New York, Macmillan Pub. Co., 1979), page 465. Italics original

direction to indulge an appetite—say, an appetite for companionship or food or sex. The satisfaction of Jesus—that is, belief in Jesus, embracing Jesus, loving Jesus, being content in Jesus—is going to be the power that severs the root of that impulse."[5]

Few of us understand how to experience Christ in this way when we first meet him. He is, however, eager to teach us. Even if it is hard to imagine that Jesus can be deeply satisfying, consider turning to him and asking him to teach you the satisfaction of knowing him. Paul considering knowing Christ more satisfying than any achievement the world had to offer. (Philippians 3:7-11) If this is true, then knowing Christ is greater than any earthly pleasure.

Lead Us Not Into Temptation

Jesus taught how important it is that we pray against temptation. Prayer draws us into the battle. In this way, praying is a matter of joining our will to the will of God. We can best deal with temptation by rising each morning and praying that God would alert us to danger, show us the way of escape, and empower us to move away from sin and toward him. Prayer is the fuel of our actions. It is not a water fountain to be sipped at occasionally but is instead the very river of life for us.

I believe in preemptive prayer. While you should surely pray in the midst of temptation, you may find more often than not that temptation will overrun you if you aren't prepared to recognize it and resist. Pray

---

5. John Piper, "How does unbelief contribute to the need I feel for pornography?", www.desiringgod.org 12/8/2009

preemptively – prepare for the attack of the day. Prepare your mind for the assault on your eyes and heart. Pray preemptively that God will fill your heart with the love of Christ who sustains us. Pray preemptively that Jesus becomes your true affection.

Lack of prayer in the life of the Christian is common. It is also deadly to the soul. If you're going to defeat sin and live for God, you must become a man of prayer. Being able to converse openly with the God of the universe is a wondrous thing. As E.M. Bounds puts it: "Prayer should not be regarded as a duty which must be performed, but rather as a privilege to be enjoyed, a rare delight that is always revealing some new beauty."[6]

Dealing with Failure

There are two ways to see failure. One is to get defeated; your failure seems like the worst thing in the world. The other is to use your failure as a learning experience. Your progress will have its better days, those days where you flirt with danger, and then too days when you fail. The real question is: what is the trend? Do you see overall improvement? Are you lusting or using pornography less frequently, for shorter periods of time? Are you spending more time in God's word? Are you moving toward others in relationship? Are you getting to the bottom of other issues in your life, such as laziness, anger, or fear? All of these are important evidence of positive growth. As the trend continues then it's progress. Progress, not perfection, is our goal.

---

6. Bounds, E. M., *Purpose in prayer*. (Fleming H. Revell Co., 1920)

Is there continued relapse without real progress? Your motivation may not be strong enough. You might be one of those people who need more of a kick in the butt. Enlist the help of a good brother to serve you in that way. Is your problem worse now that it was when you started? You are probably dealing legalistically with lust. Focus on the grace of God and enjoying fellowship with Him. If you try to do this under your own power it will definitely get worse.

Think about the seemingly unimportant decisions that led to your failure. Make a journal of the days of greatest temptation and failure. What else was happening that day? Did you get into a fight with your wife? Was there a big disappointment that happened? Were you facing a difficult decision, or a sticky situation that you were getting into? Were you afraid for the future, or remorseful about the past?

There are other kinds of triggers as well. Did you have a lot of time alone? That may be something that you need to avoid. Were you up too late and tired? You might have used porn or masturbation to wake yourself up! Journal these things, and then plan for how you will deal with those next time, and stand your ground.

What about Masturbation?

This is the question I get asked all the time: is masturbation a sin? Secular research indicates that masturbation is good for you. It can improve your immune system, build your resistance to prostate gland infection, boost your mood by releasing endorphins, and help you sleep. So if it's so good for you, why do we feel guilty about it? The first time you masturbated, did you go to your parents and tell them, "I think I've discovered a way to release endorphins, give me a sense of well-being, and keep my prostate healthy"?

Masturbation is not mentioned in the Bible. Lust, however is clearly addressed, and it's hard to have one without the other. Can you masturbate without lusting? "I made a covenant with my eyes not to look lustfully at a girl." (Job 31:1) Can you masturbate in a way that builds oneness with your spouse? Can you masturbate with a clear conscience without experiencing shame? Can you masturbate without deepening your desire to use pornography? There is a progression that often occurs with masturbation, where one thing seems to lead to another. "Then when lust has conceived, it gives birth to sin; and when sin is accomplished, it brings forth death." (James 1:15) Since sex is given for such purposes as oneness (Genesis 2:24) and intimate knowledge (Genesis 4:1), having sex with oneself seems to miss some of the significant biblical reasons for sexual intimacy. Masturbating is not what was designed for our sexuality.

Masturbation can establish a pattern of laziness. If a single man wants to have an orgasm, he needs to first become a man and undergo the hard work of courting and marrying a woman. If a married man wants to have an orgasm, he needs to first undergo the hard work of loving, leading, and romancing his wife. Lazy men are more prone to rub one out in the shower each morning rather than undergo the labors usually associated with responsible masculine married life.

According to Christian counselor Jeffrey Black,

"Masturbation is sex with yourself. If I'm having sex with myself, I don't have to invest myself in another person. People who are "addicted" to pornography aren't so much addicted to lurid material as they're addicted to self-centeredness. They're committed to serving themselves, to doing whatever they can to find a convenient way not to die to self, which is the nature of companionship in a relationship."[7]

1 Corinthians 7:4 says, "For the wife does not have authority over her own body, but the husband does. Likewise the husband does not have authority over his own body, but the wife does." A married man does not own his body, but rather he is a steward of his body that belongs to his bride and his God. Every single man, likewise, is merely a steward of his body for his God, and eventually for his bride. Consequently, a man has no right to touch himself sexually without discussing it with his wife, since it is, after all, her body he is looking after.

C. S. Lewis shows a great deal of insight on the topic of masturbation in the following quote, from a letter to a friend,

"For me the real evil of masturbation would be that it takes an appetite which, in lawful use, leads the individual out of himself to complete (and correct) his own personality in that of another (and finally in children and even grandchildren) and turns it back; sends the man back into the prison of himself, there to keep a harem of imaginary brides. And this

7. Jeffrey S. Black, "Pornography, Masturbation, and other Misuses: A Perversion of Intimacy", *Journal of Biblical Counseling*, 13:3, Spring 1995

harem, once admitted, works against his ever getting out and really uniting with a real woman. For the harem is always accessible, always subservient, calls for no sacrifices or adjustments, and can be endowed with erotic and psychological attractions which no woman can rival. Among those shadowy brides he is always adored, always the perfect lover; no demand is made on his unselfishness, no mortification ever imposed on his vanity. In the end, they become merely the medium through which he increasingly adores himself."[8]

Additionally, there is a toxic waste dump of filth in our heads, which masturbation prompts us to access. If you think that this dump doesn't leak over into the rest of your life, you are fooling yourself. Masturbation is self-worship. As long as we worship something else besides God, we will find other areas of our lives retarded.

So is masturbation a sin? Probably so for you. Is it the worst sin? Hardly. We need to take the longer wider view here, and not get discouraged. It would be a very bad thing to focus on this as a primary issue, except as the Holy Spirit is revealing it to you, and empowering you to avoid it. Any tendency to beat yourself up over failures with masturbation will not lead you closer to God.

We need to be men who are devoted to others, not ourselves. If we are married, we need to love our wives enough to give ourselves fully to them. If we are single we need to patiently trust God with our sexuality.

8. Lewis, Clive Staples, and Walter Hooper. *Collected letters: Narnia, Cambridge and Joy 1950-1963*. HarperCollins, 2007, p. 758

For Group Discussion:

Share what's been going on with you lately. Rejoice in any victories someone has had in spiritual battle, and talk about any lessons learned.

Talk about some of the things that trigger sexual sin for you. How might you deal with things like anger, frustration, fear, boredom, and loneliness in a way that is godly?

In what ways have you failed since beginning this study? How might you respond to and learn from these failures? Have you received any new insights on the nature of failure?

What do you think of the material on masturbation? Share your thoughts with one another on whether this is an important issue for you or not.

Pray for each member in your group. Give thanks to God who, even in our stumbling, always leads us in triumph in Christ.

TEN

REAL MEN, REAL RELATIONSHIPS

Life is relationships; the rest is just details.
Gary Smalley

A recent trip to a local book mega-store revealed three adjacent sections: *Love & Sex*, *Relationships*, and *Sexuality*. The first section seemed to be about dating and marriage while the last section was full of books that focused on sexual technique. Sandwiched between these was the section was on relationships. As I browsed these titles, I could see two themes: why men have a hard time understanding women and vice versa, and how we resolve this or that difficulty in our relationship. There were numerous books on dealing with cheating and infidelity, including some on how to cheat and get away with it.

This may correspond with what you already know: relationships are hard for everybody. They are especially hard for regular users of pornography. Part of being freed from your enslavement to lust is to learn to build genuine, healthy, relationships. Relationships are the source of the intimacy you have been trying to find in pornography.

Pornography and masturbation are to intimacy what cotton candy is to food. Just as cotton candy doesn't really satisfy what you're looking for when you say, "I'm hungry", pornography doesn't satisfy your deepest relational needs. In fact pornography inhibits your ability to have quality relationships because:

- Pornography divorces sexuality from any kind of genuine relationship.
- Through mental rehearsal of non-relational sex, the user increasingly becomes the object of their own love in a way that leaves less and less room for anyone else.
- Pornography trains the person who engages in it to live in his head in a world of self-gratification that excludes others, leading to isolation.
- Pornography often becomes a means of dealing with the strain of relational conflict while rendering you less able to manage it.
- Pornography keeps you in a state of adolescent selfishness, rendering them incapable of adult relating or sexual functioning, and too immature for the kind of investment that a real relationship entails.

Pornography becomes the primary relationship in life. The people in your life are judged in terms of whether they get in the way of the addiction, or encourage it. A husband or father who needs to be emotionally engaged with their spouse or children will not really do so, because their inner world of fantasy has overlaid the real one. The side effect of this is that the spouses and children of pornography addicts experience an emotional detachment that, to them, feels like rejection. This especially sets children up for lifelong issues of abandonment that will likely spur addictions in their own lives down the road, as they look to fill the void that has been left by the parent. The impact on spouses is similar, leaving them to look elsewhere for the intimacy that you are supposed to provide.

In the Beginning

Men seem to be less effective at relationships than women, a characterization that is frequently popularized on television. Regardless of whether or not this is true, relationships are difficult for both men and women. Men and women both tend to place unrealistic expectations on relationships. At the outset of a new relationship, things seem rosy: we fancy both ourselves, as well as the other person, to be more perfect than they are. We are always just a little shocked when difficulty enters a relationship, as if we expected that things would go along without a hitch. There might be a good reason for this – we were created to experience perfect relationships that satisfy us completely.

> "So God created man in His own image, in the
> image of God He created him; male and female
> He created them." (Genesis 1:27)

To be created in the image of God mostly has to do with relationships. Genesis 1 is written as poetry. Hebrew poetry uses a device known as parallelism, which is to rhyme ideas rather than words in order to give rich meaning to the poem. This passage uses what is called "affirming parallelism" where three ideas develop the same thought:

> So God created man in his own image,
>> in the image of God he created him;
>>> male and female he created them.

The fact that we are relational comes from being created in the image of God. God in three persons has perfect, enjoyable relationships within Himself. He also created us as relational people. When Adam was by himself in Eden, God observed, "It is not good that the man should be alone" (Gen. 2:18). You and I were never designed to live in isolation. We are not wired to be distant from and unaffected by the people around us. In fact, since we were created in God's likeness, desire for and participation in community is a fundamental part of our humanity. The God who made us in his likeness not only does community, he is a community! To deny this aspect of your life would literally be to deny your humanity.

Before the fall, relationships weren't marked by selfishness, but rather by joy in giving to one another. I think we remember a little of what that was like, because we still expect that kind of perfection in a relationship. We have lost the song of the Garden, and so our relationships have become marked by the discordant tones of self-interest. It is my song that I want you to sing, not yours, and not His.

In the New Testament

Have you noticed something in the structure of the letters of the New Testament? Many of them use an "indicative-imperative" approach, that is, they spend the first part of the letter teaching us what is true, and the second part of the book instructing us in what to do about it. This is certainly true of Paul's letters to the Romans, Ephesians, and Colossians. In each of those great letters we see something very similar: he tells you about the gospel of Jesus, and then he tells you how the gospel affects your life.

In each case, one of the defining characteristics of those imperative sections is a section about the community of God, the church, and relationships. Ephesians is a great example of this: in chapters 1-3 Paul tells us about the spiritual blessings we have in Christ because of His work on the cross, how we have crossed over from the kingdom of darkness and been raised up in the heavenly places with Christ by grace through faith, and how we are all one in Christ no matter what our background. Then in the second half of the letter he starts to explain how those truths should affect our lives.

> "Therefore I, the prisoner of the Lord, implore you to walk in a manner worthy of the calling with which you have been called, with all humility and gentleness, with patience, showing tolerance for one another in love, being diligent to preserve the unity of the Spirit in the bond of peace." (Ephesians 4:1-3)

Paul implores us—in the original Greek the word means beseech, exhort, appeal, call forward, so Paul is putting the strongest emphasis on this—to "walk in a manner worthy" of our calling. Every grand, amazing thing from Ephesians 1-3 describes that calling to us, and that is to become the basis for our conduct in community, in relationships. Relationships preserve the unity that the Spirit has brought about by bringing us together in Christ.

The Bible is very honest about the ways relationships can be messy and disappointing. This is not a rose-colored theology. There is no admonition to feel warm fuzzy feelings and exude plastic niceness to one another. Paul calls for humility, gentleness, patience, and forbearance. These things pre-suppose difficulty in relationships. We need humility because we suffer from the sin of pride. We need gentleness because we care more about our own agenda than others. We need patience because we expect everything to go down in our timing. We need forbearance because we think of ourselves as superior to others.

We need all of these things because we are all sinners, and if sinners are going to be in real relationships we will need to show these qualities to one another. The gospel makes all the difference here, though. We can be humble because our Lord humbled himself to the point of death on a cross for us. We can be gentle because, rather than merely destroying us in our sin, Jesus came and humbly laid his life down at the hands of our violence, while we all stood by and cried out, "Crucify! Crucify!" We can be patient because God is continually faithful to us in spite of our faithlessness. We can forbear with others because no one has put up with more offense than God.

In his classic work, The Imitation of Christ, Thomas à Kempis said,

> "If all were perfect, what should we have to suffer from others for God's sake? But God has so ordained, that we may learn to bear with one another's burdens, for there is no man without fault, no man without burden, no man sufficient to himself nor wise enough. Hence we must support

one another, console one another, mutually help, counsel, and advise, for the measure of every man's virtue is best revealed in time of adversity—adversity that does not weaken a man but rather shows what he is."[1]

So is that it? Are relationships just putting up with all the junk in one another's lives? If you think that, you've missed the point: we need to show these qualities in our relationships with one another because, once we are past our sinfulness, there is joy in knowing another person deeply, and being deeply known. If it's not good for the man to be alone, then it's sweet to be in fellowship!

Behold, how good and pleasant it is when brothers dwell in unity!
It is like the precious oil on the head, running down on the beard,
on the beard of Aaron, running down on the collar of his robes!
It is like the dew of Hermon, which falls on the mountains of Zion!
For there the LORD has commanded the blessing, life forevermore. (Psalm 133)

How do we interpret these two metaphors of the oil and the mountain? The oil is poured on extravagantly – it runs from the head to the beard to the robes. David, who had danced before the Lord, understood the divine place of extravagance. Fellowship that is experienced in unity is abundant with deep sharing, mutual enjoyment, laughter,

---

1. Thomas à Kempis, *The imitation of Christ* (Oak Harbor: Logos Research Systems), 28

and appreciation. That kind of fellowship is a picture of heaven. Mount Hermon, a snow-capped mountain in northern Israel, holds much of the life-giving water that flows down into the valley below, watering the fertile orchards on the Golan Heights, and feeding springs and streams that form the Jordan River. This is a picture of life, the kind that flows from above, like dew falling, like rain on parched ground. The life of all true fellowship flows from God.

Men and Relationships

So getting back to our original question: are there any specific reasons why men have a harder time with relationships? Is it just natural for them to relate better to cars and power tools than to women or each other? Let's go back to our verse in Genesis and read a little further:

"God created man in his own image, in the image of God he created him; male and female he created them. God blessed them and said to them, "Be fruitful and increase in number; fill the earth and subdue it. Rule over the fish of the sea and the birds of the air and over every living creature that moves on the ground." (Genesis 1:27-28)

In the same way that God moved into the chaos of what He had created and began to build order, he calls man to do the same thing. He calls him to cultivate the garden, and subdue a chaotic world around him. When God creates man, the land is untamed, but one part is orderly. God puts the man in the garden and tells him to fill and subdue – make the rest of the planet look like Eden.

Men are by nature cultivators, fixers, builders. Men like to make things, and then spend the rest of their time fixing and tuning them. Look at how men treat cars, homes, computers—they're always tinkering around, trying to get a few more RPMs out of everything. Most men are far better at fixing the plumbing than they are at relationships. The problem is that if a man doesn't love God he cultivates the wrong things: he cultivates sin and rebellion.

One of the reasons that we so easily fall into pornography is that it gives us access to a form of sexuality that seems easier than building relationships. We don't have to conquer or build or cultivate anything to get those feelings that solo sex gives us. That is also what is wrong with it: we were meant to build a relationship and lovingly win a woman before experiencing the pleasure of sex.

Larry Crabb in his book *The Silence of Adam* postulates that Adam's first sin was not to intervene between the serpent and Eve. He suggests that it is likely, or at least possible, that Adam was present as Satan spoke to his wife, but that he remained silent and allowed her to enter in to sin. He abandoned his strength for passivity.

> "God gave the responsibility to name the animals to the man, not to the woman. Eve was not yet created. Like God, man was called to speak into darkness, to move into the confusion of a completely unnamed kingdom of animals, and to assign every one a name. Could it be that God intended men to behave like him by courageously moving into whatever spheres of mystery they encounter

and speaking with imagination and life-giving power into the confusion they face?[2]

Adam and Eve were to "till and keep the garden"; that is, they were called to protect and to nurture. Strength, the opposite of violence, is in the man to guard relationships, not to destroy them. Intimacy, the opposite of lust, is in the man to nurture people, not to use them for his selfish desires. Adam's first recorded words were relational and poetic: "She is bone of my bone and flesh of my flesh."[3]

After some time of living out his divine calling, Adam failed when his wife needed him the most. That failure turned into the curse of sin, and Christ had to come to redeem us from that failure. However, the silence of Adam continues in every man, and nowhere does that show more clearly than in our relationships and sexuality. Crabb continues:

"The root problem beneath our more visible problems is that we don't strive for depth or quality in our relationships. We're not richly masculine as husbands, fathers, sons, brothers, or friends. We steer clear of those areas in our relationships that utterly baffle us, because we don't want to accept our responsibility to move without a code. Any situation that demands we move with courage confronts us with the dreaded question "Do I have

2. Larry Crabb, *The Silence of Adam*, (Grand Rapids: Zondervan), 64
3. Ibid, 75

what it takes to do what a real man is called by God to do?"[4]

Men have difficulty with relationships because we prefer it when we have a blueprint, a project plan, an algorithm for everything in life. Relationships, on the other hand, are complicated, unpredictable, and chaotic. In order to succeed, we're going to have to move in to uncomfortable waters without a map. We have to move in to relationships with the empty hands of faith, and tell God, "I don't know what to do in this situation, but I'm going in there trusting you. No matter what happens I'm going to follow you in there."

That, of course, is the place that God wants us to be. He wants us to be like his Son was, when he moved into the chaos of sinful humanity 2000 years ago. He was constantly dependent, constantly without his own plan."

> So Jesus said to them, "Truly, truly, I say to you, the Son can do nothing of his own accord, but only what he sees the Father doing. For whatever the Father does, that the Son does likewise. For the Father loves the Son and shows him all that he himself is doing. And greater works than these will he show him, so that you may marvel. (John 5:19–20)

Strategies for discovery

Building relationships with others, both men and women, is essential for change. After all, it's relational

---

4. Ibid, 106

intimacy that you've been replacing with lust and pornography, and you might as well discover the real thing.
The temptations of pornography decrease as we build
fulfilling relationships with other Christians. This may
seem a daunting task for you, especially if you consider
yourself shy and reserved. You may have never had a true
friendship. The promise of the joy of fellowship comes
to us from God who is the giver of all good gifts. He
promises us in his word that our experience of this joy
will grow as we apply ourselves to building relationships.

> Now concerning brotherly love you have no need
> for anyone to write to you, for you yourselves have
> been taught by God to love one another, for that
> indeed is what you are doing to all the brothers
> throughout Macedonia. But we urge you, brothers,
> to do this more and more. (1 Thessalonians 4:9-10)

So there is God's part in this, and there is ours — "do
this more and more." God provides the means for us to
have spiritual relationships, not based on selfish interest
or natural affinity, but serving love in response to his
love for us. He teaches us to love by loving us in Christ.
Christian love is based on the unity of the Spirit, and
anchored in God's truth, his perspective. So now that
the power of love is present in your heart, you can make
it your business to enter into deep relationships.

Here are a handful of ideas for you to get on the road
to greater personal intimacy with others:

Seek God and His kingdom first. Relational intimacy
is the by-product of getting first things first. "But seek
first His kingdom and His righteousness, and all these
things will be added to you." (Matthew 6:33) Seeking his

kingdom is not just a horizontal monastic enterprise; it is both loving God and loving others. The kingdom of God is people with Christ at the center.

Make and plan time in your life for relationship with others. If you've been spending a lot of time by yourself because of your secret life, it will take planning to replace that time. You can't just move in front of the TV and replace porn with sports and video games. Plan time in your schedule for relationships. Make it a priority. If you're involved in ministry, and you don't have time for people, then you're too busy.

Be intentional with time together. Intentional is not the same as having an agenda, which is usually focused on what I expect you to do and often is designed to make things easier for me. Instead, being intentional means you have decided to relate deeply, emotionally, sacrificially, for the good of another person, and you decide not to allow trivialities to distract from that focus

Understand the power of words. Proverbs 12:18 says "There is one who speaks rashly like the thrusts of a sword, But the tongue of the wise brings healing." Proverbs 15:4 says, "A soothing tongue is a tree of life, But perversion in it crushes the spirit." Words are powerful in both directions; we can do great harm with them, but also great good. Use your words to encourage and build up others, and you will be blessed!

Be transparent in your relationships. People are on their guard in conversation, they often don't open up easily because they're not sure how you're going to treat them if they reveal themselves. Leading with your own transparency, which includes openness about our faults and

weaknesses as well as confessing your positive feelings
about them, will generally open people up to you. If
you're in an accountability relationship, this is a great
way to learn to be transparent.

Enter in to the world of the other person. This mostly has
to do with taking an interest in the thoughts and feelings
of the other person. Learn how to ask questions that draw
another person out. If you have difficultly focusing on
conversations in public places then find a place to hang
out where you can focus on the person. You want to be
absorbed in them.

*Focus conversation on specific areas where you can involve
God in the life of the other person.* This falls into three
general areas of discovery:

- First, what is troubling you right now? What kinds
  of things are hardest? What are the low points in
  your day, or your life? You're looking for places
  where the gospel applies to them.

- Second, what are your joys, the things you are
  happiest about? You're looking to share with them
  in the opportunity of praising God together.

- Thirdly, what do you want out of life? What do
  you hope for? What are your dreams and aspira-
  tions? You're looking for the things in their life
  that you can pray about.

Value the emotional component of relationships. Look how
the Bible ties in emotional components with the actions
of God's people in relationships:

"Be kind to one another, tender-hearted, forgiving
each other, just as God in Christ also has forgiven

you." (Ephesians 4:32)

"But we proved to be gentle among you, as a nursing mother tenderly cares for her own children. Having so fond an affection for you, we were well-pleased to impart to you not only the gospel of God but also our own lives, because you had become very dear to us." (1 Thessalonians 2:7-8)

When you really seek genuine depth and quality in relationships, you discover the reason we were made in the image of God – to have intimacy with others. You will also find that the lure of pornography will lose some of its savor as you get a taste for building intimacy the way God designed it. The highest form of that intimacy is in a committed sexual relationship between a husband and wife, and that is the topic of our next chapter.

For Group Discussion

Share what's been going on with you lately. Have you discovered any triggers for sexual sin? Have you been able to apply the truth of the word in those moments?

What do you think are some of your relational strengths and weaknesses?

What are some barriers for you to implementing the strategies for moving toward relational intimacy? What might be some ways of combating those barriers?

Pray for each member in your group. Thank God for his desire to teach us to be more relational with him and others.

ELEVEN

THE PRACTICE OF DELIGHT

"Come into your garden, my love; taste its finest fruits." (Song of Solomon 4:16)

Sex is good. Sex is good because the One who made sex is good. For all the harm that has been done in the name of sex, it is still one of God's greatest gifts to us.

The goal of gaining freedom from sexual sin is not merely to stop doing something wrong. The real goal is to move toward God's design for sex—sex that is good, sex that is better than fantasizing and masturbating. In fact, I have good news for you: God wants you to have the best sex ever. Christians should have far better sex than non-Christians because we have the basis for a more perfect unity with our partner. Christians know the God who invented pleasure, and "who richly provides us with everything to enjoy." (1 Timothy 6:7)

In order to experience the joy of sex as God designed it, we need to have the kind of relationship for sex that God intended. God created men and women to enjoy sex within the commitment of marriage. By contrast the overwhelming message of our culture is that committed sexuality is boring. Newness and novelty are supposedly what makes sex exciting. I'm here to tell you that is just not true, because good sex is like playing the saxophone:

Let's say that I have never played a musical instrument in my life, but I want to learn one now. I go down to the local music store and I buy a saxophone, a method book, a music stand, and a metronome. I'm ready to go. I figure out how to make a sound on it, learn about notes and staves and rests and all that, and after 3 months I am playing *Mary Had a Little Lamb* just about as well as any 4th grader.

I then proceed to sell my saxophone and buy a trombone. The music stand and the metronome are still useful, but the trombone has a totally different embouchure, there are no keys, the music is in another clef, the slide is imprecise. Nonetheless, after another 3 months I've figured out *Mary Had a Little Lamb* again. Then, I exchange my trombone for a viola. Everything is different again: different clef, working the bow, the fingerings, etc. Next, I sell that viola and get a piano… So wait, what's my point?

Sex is like playing music; you don't enjoy it more just because you're switching instruments all the time.

Have you had plenty of sexual relationships in your past? Which of them were truly deeply satisfying? In which relationships did you become a master at love-making such that you and your partner experienced the profound joy and excitement that comes with great sex? The fact is, novelty is not able to fulfill you in the way that intimacy does.

At the time of this writing, I have been married to a wonderful Christian woman for 35 years, and I feel like I'm just starting to get the hang of it. Sex is better for us now than it was when we were younger because our relationship is better, we are closer to God, we have grown in intimacy, and we have laughed and cried and rejoiced and suffered together for a long time. That's how God designed it; intimacy should be the source of our joy together.

What does the Bible teach us about sex?

Sex is God's creation.

"And the rib that the LORD God had taken from the man he made into a woman and brought her to the man. Then the man said, "This at last is bone of my bones and flesh of my flesh; she shall be called Woman, because she was taken out of Man." Therefore a man shall leave his father and his mother and hold fast to his wife, and they shall become one flesh. And the man and his wife were both naked and were not ashamed."
(Genesis 2:22–25)

Sex existed before the Fall, and wasn't given just for procreation. They were "one flesh" – united in holy love, and they had no shame. Sex was given to the original humans for their enjoyment and satisfaction.

Sex is meant for marriage.

"You shall not commit adultery." (Exodus 20:14)

"Let marriage be held in honor among all, and let the marriage bed be undefiled, for God will judge the sexually immoral and adulterous."
(Hebrews 13:4)

"Let us behave properly as in the day, not in carousing and drunkenness, not in sexual promiscuity and sensuality, not in strife and jealousy."
(Romans 13:13)

If it's true that, during sex, two people become one flesh, then it stands to reason you can't really be "one" with more than one person. God calls any other kind of arithmetic adultery, a word that implies faithlessness and betrayal. How can you give yourself fully to someone if you know that at any minute they might give themselves to another? Have you ever been betrayed in a relationship? Most of us have. Do you know what it's like to live with the insecurity that the woman you're with might run off with someone else? There is an inherent insecurity in relationships on this side of the Fall, a lack of fundamental trust in others. None of that sense of insecurity makes for good sex, because true intimacy means sharing myself fully with another — all the barriers are down and we are naked before one another.

If you engage in pre-marital sex you are living in a world of insecurity — do you want her for her body, or do you really love her? Is she just getting back at her ex-boyfriend? Is she merely a conquest to make you feel more like a man? Without the commitment of marriage, no matter how much you may fool yourself into thinking that you'll love each other until the end of time, no one is willing to bet the ranch on it.

If you're married and you commit adultery, you engage in the plunder of souls for an orgasm, devastating those you supposedly love for the most selfish of pleasures. The pain you will cause yourself and your family is stupendous, and can take years to heal, if at all.

This is why the Bible is clear on the importance of commitment and fidelity. God designed sex, designed us, to be in a committed life-long relationship as the proper context for sex. That context is marriage.

Sex is about giving.

> "The husband should fulfill his wife's sexual needs, and the wife should fulfill her husband's needs. The wife gives authority over her body to her husband, and the husband gives authority over his body to his wife." (1 Corinthians 7:3–4, NLT)

As we've already observed, masturbation is inherently self-centered. The Bible teaches us that sex is about giving to another, not taking what you want, when you want it. To get the most out of sex in marriage, your focus should be on your wife's pleasure. The three best words a man can hear after sex are: "that was incredible!"

What if you're single? In the same way that a married man should save his body for his wife, a single man should save his body for his future wife. God is good, and He gives good things to his children – you should ask Him to show you how to do this. You can start loving your future wife right now by abstaining from taking your pleasure by yourself. In fact, that kind of commitment might also help you finish school, get a job, and find and win a good Christian woman too.

Sex is to be celebrated.

The main reason that I know that God intends for us to celebrate sex is that we have a book in the Bible that does just that, and nothing else. It's called The Song of Songs or the Song of Solomon. The Song is perhaps the most unusual book in the Bible: it has no liturgy or commandments, no hymns, oracles, or visions. There is no mention of God, grace, the temple, sacrifice, righteousness, wickedness, worship, or much of anything that could be associated with religion. The Song is, nonetheless, full of words about love and sex. In fact, this is a love poem, a sex poem, and I'm glad it's in our Bible to teach us that sex is worth celebrating.

"This is Solomon's song of songs, more wonderful than any other. Kiss me and kiss me again, for your love is sweeter than wine. How fragrant your cologne; your name is like its spreading fragrance. No wonder all the young women love you! Take me with you; come, let's run! The king has brought me into his bedroom." (Song of Solomon, 1:1-4a, NLT)

What an exciting opening line—kiss me and kiss me again! For centuries, interpreters who were embarrassed by the frank sensuality of The Song have tried to explain this collection of love poetry as portraying the relationship between Christ and the Church, but I don't know how they can get that from this.

"You are as exciting, my darling, as a mare among Pharaoh's stallions." (Song of Solomon 1:9, NLT)

I don't know how many of you have been around horses that much, but if you take a mare into a stable full of stallions, it will get quite rowdy. To put it in more modern terms, the man is saying, "you make me hot!"

"Like the finest apple tree in the orchard is my lover among other young men. I sit in his delightful shade and taste his delicious fruit. He escorts me to the banquet hall; it's obvious how much he loves me. Strengthen me with raisin cakes, refresh me with apples, for I am weak with love. His left arm

is under my head, and his right arm embraces me."
(Song of Solomon 2:3-6, NLT)

This is full of erotic imagery, and we'll explain some
of it as we go, but at this point I would recommend that
if you want to learn more about the imagery found in the
Song of Songs, you should go buy a good commentary.
My favorites are the ones by G. Lloyd Carr and Tom
Gledhill.[1]

What do we learn about sex from the Song?

There is commitment

One of the phrases that repeats in The Song is, "my
lover is mine and I am his" (cf. 2:16, 6:3). This is not
just some chance rendezvous in the barley field: it's a
committed relationship. A lot of people think that since
The Song is associated with Solomon, this would be a
hypocritical inference. After all, Solomon "had 700 wives,
princesses, and 300 concubines." (1 Kings 11:3) How
can a guy like that have anything to say about marital
fidelity? The simple fact is that The Song is not about
Solomon - the two lovers are simply literary figures, the
product of divinely inspired imagination. This is not a
history book about Solomon; it's a poem.

The lovers' commitment adds a strong sense of security to lovemaking. While they are eager to consummate
their feelings for one another, it's not the desperation
of those who know that the enjoyment will be all too
fleeting, or a hurried coupling before one of them moves

---

1. Carr, G. Lloyd. *The Song of Solomon.* (Intervarsity Press, 2009);
Gledhill, Tom. *The Message of the Song of Songs.* (Inter-Varsity Press,
1994)

on to the next partner. There is time enough for love, because there will be love for a lifetime. The security and permanence of their relationship becomes the basis for the enjoyment of their sexual exploration of one another.

There is restraint.

At the end of three of the major sections of The Song, there is a closing adjuration:

> "Promise me, O women of Jerusalem, [by the gazelles and wild deer], not to awaken love until the time is right." (Song of Solomon 2:7; 3:5; 8:4)

In each case it is the woman who is speaking, and it each case she tells us that sex is best when it takes place in its proper context. There is a right time and place for sex; we should trust God that this gift will be provided abundantly at the right time and place. By taking matters into our own hands, we are reducing our pleasure, taking for ourselves a cheap substitute for the real enjoyment of sex.

There is more to it than this, though. Sex is best enjoyed when it is anticipated with great patience. It's not just hurried humping, the kind of rushed sex scene that Hollywood dishes out, where the lovers' hands touch at the same time on the last plate while doing the dishes together, and next thing you know, everything is swept off the table in a crash and the dining furniture is put to its most strenuous test ever.

Instead, the Song describes a celebration of the whole person. Unlike porn, it is a multi-sensory experience—they rejoice in seeing, hearing, touching, kissing, smelling, fondling, caressing, and finally having sex with one another. It's based in the relationship that they have, a fondness for one another that goes way beyond the physical. This is perhaps best understood by looking at their amazing descriptions of one another.

There is mutual appreciation.

Throughout The Song the lovers describe one another in poetic terms: each attribute is likened to something else, usually something in nature. Though we may find some of these metaphors odd, there is an important point to them: together they show appreciation for the whole person. In his commentary on the Song of Songs, Duane Garret says:

> "They relish their pleasure in each other not only with physical action, but with carefully composed words. Love is, above all, a matter of the mind and heart and should be declared. The lesson for the reader is that he or she needs to speak often and openly of his or her joy in the beloved, the spouse. This is, for many lovers, a far more embarrassing revelation of the self than anything that is done with the body. But it is precisely here that the biblical ideal of love is present—in the uniting of the bodies and hearts of the husband and wife in a bond that is as strong as death. Many homes would be happier if men and women would simply speak of their love for one another a little more often."[2]

---

2. Duane Garrett, *Proverbs, Ecclesiastes, Song of Solomon*, The New American Commentary (Nashville: Broadman & Holman, 1993), 379

It is these "carefully composed words" that are the messages we determine to send to our wives that awaken and arouse their love and passion. So much of our communication is carelessly composed. Once our wife becomes familiar to us, we stop communicating our appreciation. We come home from work, move to the stack of mail that came in the door, or get on our email to read all the very important things that others have written us. Perhaps we grunt at our wives or talk about something purely functional.

Instead, we should have already been thinking about how we could honor our wives with our words on the drive home. Upon arriving, we walk past the mail (and your false lover the computer) to her: to embrace her, to speak words of encouragement to her, to ask about her day, her feelings, totally absorbed in her world, forsaking our own to speak carefully composed words of appreciation.

This is what the two lovers do for each other in the Song. These words cherish, honor, appreciate, and they're highly erotic at times, but they are never explicit or pornographic.

> "You have captured my heart, my treasure, my bride. You hold it hostage with one glance of your eyes, with a single jewel of your necklace. Your love delights me, my treasure, my bride. Your love is better than wine, your perfume more fragrant than spices. Your lips are as sweet as nectar, my bride. Honey and milk are under your tongue. Your clothes are scented like the cedars of Lebanon. You are my private garden, my treasure, my

bride, a secluded spring, a hidden fountain. Your
thighs shelter a paradise of pomegranates with rare
spices—You are a garden fountain, a well of fresh
water streaming down from Lebanon's mountains."
(4:9-15, NLT)

The lovers are very creative in their compliments of
one another. I like what C.J. Mahaney says about this in
John Piper's Sex and the Supremacy of Christ

"This is miles away from simple chit-chat, or prac-
ticalities like kids, carpools, and church meetings.
This is a category of communication set apart from
the stuff of daily life, reserved for a unique and
wonderful purpose. It is highly intentional, creative, provocative, erotic language. Its purpose is
to arouse romantic passion—to inflame, slowly and
intentionally, all the while honoring and delighting
one's spouse."[3]

"How beautiful are your sandaled feet, O queenly
maiden. Your rounded thighs are like jewels, the
work of a skilled craftsman. Your navel is perfectly
formed like a goblet filled with mixed wine. Between
your thighs lies a mound of wheat bordered with
lilies. Your breasts are like two fawns, twin fawns of
a gazelle. Your neck is as beautiful as an ivory tower.
Your eyes are like the sparkling pools in Heshbon
by the gate of Bath-rabbim. Your nose is as fine
as the tower of Lebanon overlooking Damascus.

3. C.J. Mahaney, "Sex, Romance, and the Glory of God: What every
Christian husband needs to know", Sex and the Supremacy of Christ, ed.
John Piper, (Wheaton, IL: Crossway Books, 2005), 157

Your head is as majestic as Mount Carmel, and the sheen of your hair radiates royalty. The king is held captive by its tresses. Oh, how beautiful you are! How pleasing, my love, how full of delights! You are slender like a palm tree, and your breasts are like its clusters of fruit. I said, "I will climb the palm tree and take hold of its fruit." May your breasts be like grape clusters, and the fragrance of your breath like apples. May your kisses be as exciting as the best wine, flowing gently over lips and teeth." (7:1-9, NLT)

The thing to notice here is not how weird some of these metaphors may sound to us, but to look at the creativity involved in writing these similes. He's not just saying, "I like your boobs." Instead, he uses poetic language that shows both his appreciation for her and the effect that she has on him. The speaker doesn't merely find some analogue for each of her physical features; he also describes his own feelings for her as well as his growing desire for her. Even in describing her physical features you note how thorough he is—he loves the whole person, her eyes, lips, nose, navel, thighs, neck, hair, teeth—nothing is left out, including those amazing grape clusters. It's more than just acknowledging that your wife has all the equipment in good shape; it's voicing your appreciation of her as a whole person.

Righteousness, Relationship, and Romance

You can save your money on all those "how to get a woman into bed" books. There are really three key things that will stir up the flame of passion in a woman: your walk with God, your relational depth, and the romance that you bring to the relationship. "Righteousness, relationship, and romance" are just alliteration for these three qualities. If you're married and you want to build the passion in your marriage, or if you're single and want to know what qualities women are looking for, this is it!

Nothing is sexier than someone who is close to God. Your devotion to the Lord demonstrates to your wife that your heart is caught up and captured by greater things than yourself.

There is no greater aphrodisiac than prayer. Praying with your wife (you single guys are allowed to do this with your girlfriends as well) is a great way to build closeness with each other as you build it with the Lord. Invite your wife to go up to the bed and get naked together (singles, sorry, this part is not for you) and pray with her. Don't rush – focus on glorifying God. You can thank Him for the gift of your wife, for the gift of sex, for the oneness that He has created. You should be the initiator of prayer in your relationship. Don't passively wait for her to bring it up. A woman likes to be pursued, to be caught up and swept off her feet. Why not sweep her off her feet and carry her to the throne of grace?

Intimate relating increases sexual desire. As a man, you're designed to be more visual; seeing a woman's naked body is sexier to you than seeing into her soul. Women are designed differently – it is your soul that they want to you to share. For you, uncovering your nakedness is letting her see the real you, and taking a profound interest in her thoughts and feelings. It may be difficult for you at first, but in time you will enjoy being this kind of naked with her, and it will enhance uncovering her physical nakedness.

Romancing your wife tells her that she is special, that she is worth the investment of your time to romance. What strikes me the most as I read through the Song of Solomon is the level of detail of each one's praise for the other person. This is no minimum effort. Have you ever thought about all the things that you love about your wife? Have you ever listed them out? Have you ever made a song about it? Now that would be romantic, at least to her.

Maybe you're not quite up to the song-writing thing, but how about planning a surprise outing, or sending an email or text from work telling her that you were thinking of her? Why not set aside a night that is totally devoted to her enjoyment? Why not buy a very small gift for her, something simple and even everyday, and give it to her on a day that's not an occasion? It says, "I was thinking of you, and I saw this and got it for you." Her favorite hand cream on any Tuesday can be more romantic than a dozen roses on your anniversary, because you were thinking of her when you didn't have to be.

While this is the briefest of sections on this topic, I'd like to recommend another book here. Get a copy of Sex and the Supremacy of Christ, edited by John Piper. Get it now, and read it twice.

Final Thoughts

Great, healthy, rewarding sex is God's will for you, and you should be enjoying it to the fullest. We've come a long way in the last eleven chapters. My goal has been to prepare you to "walk in a manner worthy" of the sexuality you've been called to by God. I hope the journey so far has been rewarding, and that you will never give up. Even if you have some setbacks, don't worry – God is faithful, and He will see you through to the other side. Keep reminding yourself:

"He who began a good work in you will perfect it until the day of Christ Jesus." (Philippians 1:6)

Speaking of the other side of eternity, let's finish by taking our story to where it's really going.

For Group Discussion

Share what's been going on with you lately. Have you gained any insights into your relationships with others? Have you been more intentional in going deep in relating?

What are some negative words you've heard to describe sex? How do you think God's description of sexuality would differ from these descriptions?

In what ways have incorrect views of sexuality entered your thinking? How do they connect with your problems in sexual sin and pornography? How might incorporating God's view affect your struggle with sexual sin?

*In what ways might **not** having commitment, restraint, and mutual appreciation harm a relationship? What might it be life to have a sexual relationship with those components present?*

Pray for each member in your group. Thank God for the gift of sex, and ask him to prepare you to be a godly, commitment partner in marriage.

Twelve

Our Future Hope

One of the things that I hear fairly often is this question: when is it going to get easier? When will I no longer struggle with lust? When will the impulse to use pornography, or masturbate go away? Does it get better? Will I ever be really free?

The truth is that you likely will struggle with lust for the rest of your life. Some days will be easier while other days will be harder. Sin does not go away. As we discussed in earlier chapters, the Bible teaches that our old self (the one controlled by sin) decays and becomes more corrupt over time: "your old self… is being corrupted by its deceitful desires." (Ephesians 4:22, NIV) That seems like a depressing thought – things seem to be getting worse, instead of better.

There is so much more to the story: the new self is "created to be like God in true righteousness and holiness." (Ephesians 4:24, NIV) Even though the *presence* of the corrupted old self will never be fully displaced, its ruling *power* has been broken. As a result, we can live more and more in the power of the new life of the Spirit planted within us. As we do so, God transforms us into the person He intended us to be, and prepares us for a fantastic future. That future finds its fullness in heaven when we are reunited with God.

This is the thing that has made the biggest difference in my outlook on the struggle with sin: the hope of heaven. In heaven, we will not suffer, we will not be tempted by lust, we will not sin—we won't even want to. Heaven is our true home. We will be so thoroughly satisfied by heaven that the very thought of sin will be abhorrent to us.

My goal in this chapter is to encourage you to live radically sacrificial lives in light of your place in salvation history. The Christian life is one of one of joy and satisfaction and adventure. That joy and satisfaction is experienced in the context of hard work, struggle, and even suffering.

The victorious Christian life is glorifying Christ as we join him in his mission for this world. He is at work calling lost people to Himself. We participate through preaching the gospel and living the same gospel. What will really break the power of sin in your life is to start living for God. What makes it all worth it is the reward of heaven.

Heaven

C.S. Lewis believed that our earthly desires are in fact desires for heaven. Because we are living in a broken world, those desires have nothing else to attach themselves to except what is available here:

> "Now, if we are made for heaven, the desire for our proper place will be already in us, but not yet attached to the true object, and will even appear as the rival of that object... The books or the music in which we thought the beauty was located will betray us if we trust to them; it was not in them, it only came through them, and what came through

them was longing. These things—the beauty, the memory of our own past—are good images of what we really desire; but if they are mistaken for the thing itself they turn into dumb idols, breaking the hearts of their worshippers. For they are not the thing itself; they are only the scent of a flower we have not found, the echo of a tune we have not heard, news from a country we have never yet visited."[1]

Many Christians have what I call an "over-realized eschatology." This is a fancy way of saying that most of us expect heaven here on earth.[2] Having a taste of the presence and power of God, we expect our lives to be free of difficulty and struggle. We see this especially in the Western church in its quest for materialism and comfort, as well as in our attitudes about sin. We get discouraged when things are hard for us because we believe that we should be able to go through life without difficulty and struggle.

In truth, heaven is where we will see the death of sin, the death of fear, lust, and strife. We will be changed completely into the people we were meant to be. Our desires will be transformed and we will no longer desire that which we don't have. Ultimately, we will experience a joy that we can't even imagine right now. So why does that matter to you right now? *We are called to live in the light of heaven.* The hope of eternal life and the rewards

1. Lewis, C.S. The Weight of Glory. Preached originally as a sermon in the Church of St Mary the Virgin, Oxford, on June 8, 1942: published in THEOLOGY, November, 1941, and by the S.P.C.K, 1942
2. Eschatology is the Biblical study of the last days, and heaven.

that are promised to us are supposed to keep us on our
feet. We live "in hope of eternal life, which God, who
never lies, promised before the ages began." (Titus 1:2)

Peter rejoiced as he looked forward to the hope of
heaven:

> "Blessed be the God and Father of our Lord Jesus
> Christ! According to his great mercy, he has caused
> us to be born again to a living hope through the
> resurrection of Jesus Christ from the dead, to an
> inheritance that is imperishable, undefiled, and
> unfading, kept in heaven for you, who by God's
> power are being guarded through faith for a sal-
> vation ready to be revealed in the last time. In
> this you rejoice, though now for a little while, if
> necessary, you have been grieved by various trials,
> so that the tested genuineness of your faith—more
> precious than gold that perishes though it is tested
> by fire—may be found to result in praise and
> glory and honor at the revelation of Jesus Christ. "
> (1 Peter 1:3–7)

We have an inheritance in heaven — what is it like?
Peter says three things that give us hope: it's imperishable,
undefiled, and unfading. That means our inheritance is
permanent, perfect in holiness, and won't fade away. He
also says that by God's power we are being guarded by
faith. It is our faith in God's power that guards us from
the corruption of this evil age, and prepares our hearts
for that final revelation of our inheritance.

It is our faith in our future hope that guards our hearts.
How do I keep from looking to the idols of this world
for fulfillment? It's because I wait in faith for the rewards

of the world to come.

I was deeply affected by a verse from the Psalms recently — "So even to old age and gray hairs, O God, do not forsake me, until I proclaim your might to another generation, your power to all those to come. " (Psalm 71:18) Instead of living for the American dream of materialistic ease, comfort, and uselessness, I can live a meaningful life in the service of others, passing on to another generation what Christ has shown me about his gospel.

What is important to know about heaven?

The first thing to realize about heaven, as we've seen, is that we are not in heaven yet.

We won't find heaven in things, or other people; we won't find it when we retire to that condo on the Gulf coast; we won't find it in that perfect romance; we only find it when we've died in Christ, or when Christ returns. This helps us in realistically appraising all the things in life this side of heaven. Every time you are tempted to find heaven in something good on this fallen earth, you can remind yourself that this is not your true home, just an echo of what God has in store for you.

The second thing is that heaven is about Jesus.

Though heaven will be full of relationships and experiences, it's not really about spending time with your lost loved ones, or meeting famous people. Heaven is about the deepest kind of fellowship with the one who redeemed us – it's all about the Lamb who was slain.

Some years ago I was reading *God is the Gospel* by John

Piper, and a question that he asked in that book struck me:

> "The critical question for our generation—and for
> every generation— is this: If you could have heaven,
> with no sickness, and with all the friends you ever
> had on earth, and all the food you ever liked, and
> all the leisure activities you ever enjoyed, and all
> the natural beauties you ever saw, all the physical
> pleasures you ever tasted, and no human conflict
> or any natural disasters, could you be satisfied with
> heaven, if Christ were not there?"[3]

We tend to think of heaven in terms of leisure, friendship, freedom from suffering, and pleasure. This is good, because those things are true. But what makes life in eternity worth it is the fact that the infinite-personal God become man will be there with us, loving us, sharing his life with us. We will be with Jesus in all his glory. We will experience a relationship with him that is so intimate, that it is called a marriage between Jesus and us. Listen to John's description:

> ". . .for the marriage of the Lamb has come, and
> his Bride has made herself ready; it was granted
> her to clothe herself with fine linen, bright and
> pure"— for the fine linen is the righteous deeds
> of the saints. And the angel said to me, "Write this:
> Blessed are those who are invited to the marriage
> supper of the Lamb." And he said to me, "These
> are the true words of God." " (Revelation 19:6–9,
> see also Isa. 62:1-5)

---

3. John Piper, *God is the Gospel: meditations on God's love as the gift of himself.* (Crossway Books, 2005), 15

The third thing that is important about heaven is that we shall be like Christ.

> "Beloved, we are God's children now, and what we will be has not yet appeared; but we know that when he appears we shall be like him, because we shall see him as he is." (1 John 3:2)

In the same way that Jesus is glorified and has a glorified body, we also will be transformed to be like him (Philippians 3:12). We will have bodies that do not wear out, perfect in every way, impervious to disease, not weak but powerful, and our hearts will be completely aligned with Jesus. God told us about our future *so that it would affect our present*. He calls us to live in a hard world with the hope of the reward that we will receive from his hand (John 14:2-3; Colossians 3:24). This makes the difficulties of this life, which is incredibly short when viewed from the standpoint of eternity, worth enduring. We are not supposed to love this world; we are supposed to eagerly expect the next one.

Eager expectancy

> "And just as it is appointed for man to die once, and after that comes judgment, so Christ, having been offered once to bear the sins of many, will appear a second time, not to deal with sin but to save those who are eagerly waiting for him." (Hebrews 9:27-28)

If we're honest, we must admit that most of us are not eagerly waiting for the return of Christ. I suspect that the reason is that we like this world. We like it a lot. In

America we go to health clubs, and take vitamins and fish oil and baby aspirin and fiber so that we can stay on this planet as long as possible. Do you look forward to Jesus calling you home? Listen with your heart to what John reveals to us in the book of Revelation, and see if this is what you were looking for: the dwelling of God with us.

> "Then I saw a new heaven and a new earth, for the first heaven and the first earth had passed away, and there was no longer any sea. I saw the Holy City, the new Jerusalem, coming down out of heaven from God, prepared as a bride beautifully dressed for her husband. And I heard a loud voice from the throne saying, "Now the dwelling of God is with men, and he will live with them. They will be his people, and God himself will be with them and be their God. He will wipe every tear from their eyes. There will be no more death or mourning or crying or pain, for the old order of things has passed away." He who was seated on the throne said, "I am making everything new!" Then he said, "Write this down, for these words are trustworthy and true." He said to me: "It is done. I am the Alpha and the Omega, the Beginning and the End. To him who is thirsty I will give to drink without cost from the spring of the water of life." (Revelation 21:1-6)

This is what our hearts really yearn for: not just the absence of "death or mourning or crying or pain," but also the positive, life-giving presence of God with us. The voice heralds what we have been seeking all along, though we have pursued that satisfaction in other things:

Jesus will be with us.

In 1952, Florence Chadwick, the first woman to swim across the English Channel in both directions, attempted to swim the 26 miles between Catalina Island and the California coastline. The water was extremely cold, and the fog was dense. After about 15 hours Florence asked to be pulled into the boat, unable to see the coastline due to the fog. As she sat in the boat, she found out she had stopped swimming less than half a mile away from her destination. She later said, "All I could see was the fog. I think if I could have seen the shore, I would have made it."[4]

How does this story relate to us? Even though the fog of our sin and the darkness surrounds us, if we could just see what heaven is, even to spend a few minutes there, our path in this world would change forever. Think about it this way: all goodness, all delight, all pleasure is derivative, that is to say, anything good, anything pleasurable, anything that fills us with delight is merely derived from something that God has made. All goodness comes from him. (James 1:17) If we were to see *real* goodness, expounded into all the glory of heaven, we would no longer want to worship the things of this world. We would see everything from the perspective of the glory of Christ. We should look forward to that, every day.

Patience

"For I consider that the sufferings of this present time are not worth comparing with the glory that is to be revealed to us. For the creation waits

---

4. Two months later, Chadwick tried again. This time was different. The same thick fog set in, but she made it because she said that she kept a mental image of the shoreline in her mind while she swam.

with eager longing for the revealing of the sons of God. For the creation was subjected to futility, not willingly, but because of him who subjected it, in hope that the creation itself will be set free from its bondage to corruption and obtain the freedom of the glory of the children of God. For we know that the whole creation has been groaning together in the pains of childbirth until now. And not only the creation, but we ourselves, who have the firstfruits of the Spirit, groan inwardly as we wait eagerly for adoption as sons, the redemption of our bodies. For in this hope we were saved. Now hope that is seen is not hope. For who hopes for what he sees? But if we hope for what we do not see, we wait for it with patience." (Romans 8:18–25)

Patience doesn't come easily to any of us. Part of that is natural, especially when it comes to our desire for another world. As C.S. Lewis said, we must be "made for another world."[5] In everyday life, perhaps the problem with patience is the uncertainty of what we are waiting for.

When my grandson Milo was born, we sat for hours and hours as my daughter Leah labored for over a day. It was hard to be patient because we didn't know when he would be born, or if he and my daughter were going to be all right. It was that uncertainty that made patience so hard for Leslie and I. With heaven it's different: the timing may be uncertain, but the assurance of heaven is not. Heaven is a promise from God the he will keep, and if you trust in Christ for your salvation, you can count on

---

5. C. S. Lewis, *Mere Christianity*: a revised and amplified edition. (HarperCollins, 2001), 137

the fact that you will be there. This is what Paul means by "hope." Hope in this world always has uncertainty, but hope in God does not. It's absolutely certain.

So we are called to be patient. Patience for us doesn't just involve waiting; it also involves not trying to build or find heaven on earth. Rather than try to set up a cheap copy of heaven here, with our materialistic dreams of worldly entertainment and comfort seeking, we are called to look to our real reward, and serve others with our lives.

Endurance

"Therefore, since we are surrounded by so great a cloud of witnesses, let us also lay aside every weight, and sin which clings so closely, and let us run with endurance the race that is set before us, looking to Jesus, the founder and perfecter of our faith, who for the joy that was set before him endured the cross, despising the shame, and is seated at the right hand of the throne of God." (Hebrews 12:1–2)

As we eagerly await the joys of heaven, along with patience comes endurance. There is the suffering of being plagued by our own sin, and the sins of others. There is the suffering of rejection from a culture that doesn't understand your devotion to God. There is the suffering of giving your life in service to others. There is a race to be run, and it requires endurance.

I think that for many of us who struggle with sexual temptations, endurance is the thing we lack most. Life is hard, and we want relief, but rather than wait on the promise of God we turn to the false promises of pornography, fantasy, and masturbation. Our relief is momentary, and usually followed by remorse, but we don't want to endure the pain of self-denial; we want it now.

If you've decided to stop using porn, you will endure suffering; it won't be easy for you. But, as you focus on the day when Christ himself will fulfill all of your deepest desires, the power of that temptation will fade. Jesus himself was tempted, but he "endured the cross, despising the shame," and the reason that the Bible gives is that is was for "the joy set before him." Christ endured suffering, shame, disappointment, and temptation without faltering because of the joy he would experience as he spent eternity with you. You can trust him that it's worth the wait.

Urgency

> "Therefore, preparing your minds for action, and being sober-minded, set your hope fully on the grace that will be brought to you at the revelation of Jesus Christ." (1 Peter 1:13)

So what is that race to be run that the passage in Hebrews just mentioned? It's the race to accomplish in this life all the things that makes the next life worth it. Peter calls us into action; there is work to be done. This world system, the *kosmos*, is evil, but the world is also full of people that Christ died to save. We have been given the task of taking the gospel to all nations (Matt 28:19), to preach the gospel near and far, and to build up the body of Christ. This isn't just the job of missionaries and paid clergy; it's a calling that belongs to the whole of Christ's body, the church.

This calling is yours from God, and every day brings you closer to the end of your life. That should fill you

with a sense of urgency. How can you live for this world
when so many are dying in their sins? How can you fritter
away the hours with television, and video games, and all
the endless forms of diversion the world has, when men
and women that you care about will go to hell, people
that you can share Christ with?

Paul was acutely aware of how short the time of his
life was, and tried to impress the same thing on us:

> "Besides this you know that the time, that the hour
> has come for you to wake from sleep. For salvation
> is nearer to us now than when we first believed.
> The night is far gone; the day is at hand. So then
> let us cast off the works of darkness and put on
> the armor of light. Let us walk properly as in the
> daytime, not in orgies and drunkenness, not in
> sexual immorality and sensuality, not in quarrel-
> ing and jealousy. But put on the Lord Jesus Christ,
> and make no provision for the flesh, to gratify its
> desires." (Romans 13:11–14)

You are running out of time, no matter whether you
have eighty years left or just a few days. You don't know
how much time you have left. Now is the time to rise
up from the chair, close the lid on the laptop, and get
into the battle. Now is the time for Christian men to live
for dangerous adventure, and work hard to build up the
church, and spread Christ's love to a lost world.

Here's how John describes a compelling scene in
heaven:

> And they sang a new song, saying, "Worthy are
> you to take the scroll and to open its seals, for you
> were slain, and by your blood you ransomed people

for God from every tribe and language and people and nation, and you have made them a kingdom and priests to our God, and they shall reign on the earth." (Rev. 5:9-10)

This song would never be sung unless people are brought into the kingdom of the Lamb who was slain. You have a role in making this song a reality, in sharing Christ with your friends, your neighbor, your co-worker, your family, or even someone you just met in the market or at a coffee bar. You have a role in teaching and discipling others. You have a role in "proclaim[ing] the excellencies of him who called you out of darkness into his marvelous light." (1 Peter 2:9)

Heaven teaches us that our time is short. "Look carefully then how you walk, not as unwise but as wise, making the best use of the time, because the days are evil." (Ephesians 5:15–16) We should feel that sense of urgency, and awake from the slumber of comfort. We are in the middle of a war, a spiritual battle, and we are all participants. This is no time for resting.

Conclusion

So why should you kick the porn habit? Is it simply to be a better person, a better husband or father, simply to have a happier, more righteous life? Those are great things, but the perhaps the best reason to lay aside the sin that so easily entangles us is that we are in a race against time. People all over the world are hungry for the good news that Christ brings. Even with all the struggle and hardship, it's an exciting race, and if the encumbrance of sin is holding you back, you can lay it aside.

C'mon! You want to get into the race, so lay porn aside, and head for the finish line.

> "Now to him who is able to keep you from stumbling and to present you blameless before the presence of his glory with great joy, to the only God, our Savior, through Jesus Christ our Lord, be glory, majesty, dominion, and authority, before all time and now and forever. Amen." (Jude 24–25)

For Group Discussion

Share how your life has changed since you started meeting together. What has God shown you? Has the power of sexual sin been substantially affected by your commitment?

As you've read though this book and discussed sexual sin and pornography, what types of things have given you hope? How can the hope of heaven help with the here and now?

In what ways do you think sustained, substantial victory over sexual sin and pornography will affect your life, especially relationally with God and others?

Reflect on the time you have spent reading this book. What are a few "take-away" points that you can incorporate into your thoughts and actions going forward?

Pray for each member in your group. Thank God for how he is going to lead each one of you as you go forward with him.

BIBLIOGRAPHY

There are many resources that have been helpful in the development of this book, and others whose opinions I have at least considered, if not accepted entirely. The following is not an endorsement of every text, but each has had something to contribute.

Jerry Bridges
    The Discipline of Grace, NavPress
    The Gospel for Real Life, NavPress

Patrick Carnes
    In the Shadows of the Net, Hazelden;
    Out of the Shadows: Understanding Sexual Addiction, Hazelden;
    Don't Call it Love: Recovery from Sexual Addiction, Bantam;
    Contrary to Love: Helping the Sexual Addict, Hazelden

G. Lloyd Carr
    The Song of Solomon, Intervarsity Press

Larry Crabb
    The Silence of Adam, Zondervan

Donna Freitas
    Sex and the Soul: juggling sexuality, spirituality, romance, and religion on America's college campuses, Oxford University Press

Tim Alan Gardner
    Sacred Sex, WaterBrook

Duane Garrett
    Proverbs, Ecclesiastes, Song of Solomon: The New American Commentary, Broadman & Holman

Tom Gledhill
The Message of the Song of Songs, Inter-Varsity Press

Norman Grubb
Continuous Revival, CLC Publications

C. S. Lewis
The Screwtape Letters, Macmillan

D. Martyn Lloyd-Jones
Revival, Pickering and Inglis Ltd.
Spiritual Depression: its causes and cure, Wm. B. Eerdmans
Publishing

Richard Lovelace
Dynamics of Spiritual Life, Intervarsity Press

Martin Luther
Commentary on Galatians, Fleming Revell

Dennis McCallum
*Satan and His Kingdom: What the Bible Says and How It Matters
to You*, Bethany House

John Murray
Redemption Accomplished and Applied, Eerdmans

Watchman Nee
Love Not the World, Christian Literature Crusade

John Owen
Of the Mortification of Sin in Believers (1656),
Of Temptation: The Nature and Power of It (1658), from Works,
volume 6

Pamela Paul
Pornified, New York, Henry Holt and Cie., 2005

Bill Perkins
When Good Men are Tempted, Zondervan, 1997

John Piper
Sex and the Supremacy of Christ, Crossway Books;
God is the Gospel: meditations on God's love as the gift of himself,
Crossway Books

Lois Mowday Rabey
The Snare, Navpress

Tamara Penix Sbraga and William T. O'Donohue
The Sex Addiction Workbook, New Harbinger

Harry W. Schaumburg
False Intimacy: Understanding the Struggle of Sexual Addiction,
Navpress,

Chuck Smith
Effective prayer life, The Word for Today

John Stott
The Cross of Christ, Inter-Varsity Press

William M. Struthers
Wired for Intimacy: How pornography hijacks the male brain,
Inter-Varsity Press

Various
Pornography: Driving the Demand in International Sex Trafficking,
Captive Daughters Media

Ed Welch
Addictions: A Banquet in the Grave, Presbyterian & Reformed
Pub. Co.

CPSIA information can be obtained
at www.ICGtesting.com
Printed in the USA
FFOW04n1506071213
2583FF

9 780984 033508